# Teens' Guide to Health and Mental Wellness

A Teen Wellness Journal For Healthy Living, Mastering Emotions and Mental Fitness

PickWood Publishing

© **Copyright 2023 - All rights reserved.**

The content contained within this book may not be reproduced, duplicated or transmitted without direct written permission from the author or the publisher.

Under no circumstances will any blame or legal responsibility be held against the publisher, or author, for any damages, reparation, or monetary loss due to the information contained within this book, either directly or indirectly.

Legal Notice:

This book is copyright protected. It is only for personal use. You cannot amend, distribute, sell, use, quote or paraphrase any part, or the content within this book, without the consent of the author or publisher.

Disclaimer Notice:

Please note the information contained within this document is for educational and entertainment purposes only. All effort has been executed to present accurate, up to date, reliable, complete information. No warranties of any kind are declared or implied. Readers acknowledge that the author is not engaged in the rendering of legal, financial, medical or professional advice. The content within this book has been derived from various sources. Please consult a licensed professional before attempting any techniques outlined in this book.

By reading this document, the reader agrees that under no circumstances is the author responsible for any losses, direct or indirect, that are incurred as a result of the use of the information contained within this document, including, but not limited to, errors, omissions, or inaccuracies.

# Contents

Trigger Warning     1

Introduction     3
    Feeling Great, Mind and Body
    An Urgent Need

1. What Do We Mean by Mental Health?     14
    A Picture of (Mental) Health
    The Forces Against You
    Be Your Own Diagnostician
    Get Support
    Fight the Statistics

2. Physical Help For Mental Health     33
    The Ingredients for Mental Wellness
    Why Exercise Makes You Feel Good
    A Weighty Issue
    How to Start Exercising
    Yoga for Mental Health

3. Overcoming Anxiety     54
    What Anxiety Feels Like
    Generation A (is for Anxiety)

    Easy Come, Easy Go
    Anxiety First Aid

4. Handling Stress                                                   70

    A Helpful Mechanism Backfires
    When Stress is in Control
    Stick to the Plan
    How to Let It Go

5. Dealing With Depression                   85
    More Than Just Feeling Sad
    Causes and Symptoms

    Once You Ask For Help
    Supporting Yourself and Your Friends

6. Bad Coping Strategies                       103
    A Question of Control
    Behaviors to Avoid
    A Vicious Circle

7. Building Your Wellness Toolbox        118
    Talking Helps
    Behavioral Therapies
    Cognitive Behavioral Therapy

    Dialectical Behavioral Therapy
    Alternative Therapies and Medicines
    How to Help Yourself

8. The Importance of Hobbies                144
    How to Keep Your Mental Health in Good Shape
    Let's Find You a Hobby!

9. Recognizing Warning Signs              150
    You're Not a Mind Reader
    Checking In Checklist

    Keeping Up Momentum

A Final Word                               159
   Free books you may find interesting...

About the Author                           163

Dedication                                 166

Resources                                  168
   Well-Being Directory

References                                 174

# Trigger Warning

This book obviously deals with mental health and all the good and bad days that that can bring. When examining ways that low mental health can make you feel, there are mentions of feeling hopeless and worthless that might resonate with some readers. It also briefly mentions suicide.

Chapter six examines some of the ways that people try to deal with feeling bad, and this chapter includes references to self-harm, eating disorders, and substance abuse. These coping mechanisms are described in a non-judgmental way and the reader is provided with clear information about why they don't work and given suggestions about what to do instead. There is no encouragement of these practices and no shaming.

# Introduction

THIS GENERATION OF TEENAGERS and young people has the worst mental health of any generation since we started keeping track. It's not surprising that you're all anxious and depressed—you're dealing with the aftermath of a global financial meltdown, a continuing pandemic, several wars, unchecked climate change, school shootings, knife crime, and an increase in sexual assaults. According to the American Psychological Association (as reported in Akers, 2022), cases of depression in teens ages 14-17 rose by 60% between 2009 and 2017. Suicide is now one of the top three causes of death for 15- to 19-year-olds according to the Centers for Disease Control and Prevention (Centers for Disease Control and Prevention, 2019). How did we get into this situation?

On the upside, generation Z is also the best generation so far at opening up about their mental health problems, talking about what is upsetting them, and is the generation most likely to speak up and get help. You guys might have more things to worry about, but you're also really open to learning how to manage all those triggers, which is great because having unattended mental health problems as a teenager means you're up to 10 times more likely to suffer from mental health problems as an adult (Murdoch Children's Media, 2021).

During puberty, your brain and your body have to go through a lot of huge changes and this can throw your whole world into turmoil. Mood changes, identity crises, and a whole lot of mental rewiring can make you feel like you are a different person every day. No wonder your mental health can take a toll. Also, some mental health disorders have very similar symptoms to normal teenage rebellion—being irritable, feeling sleepy all the time, and excessively worrying, for example—so it can be difficult to tell whether you will grow out of it or whether you need to get treatment. If you are finding it difficult to make it through a normal day because of low mental health symptoms, it's always worth talking to a professional who can help you—your family doctor, a school counselor, or an adult volunteer on a number of phone lines will be able to offer advice.

I know from experience how helpful talking to someone can be. When I was a young adult, mental health wasn't something we talked about. In fact, if you did mention that you were struggling, it was often viewed as a sign of weakness, and you'd get teased for it. This was even more true when I joined the police force as a teenage cadet. We were expected to get on and deal with anything and everything we came across, and that included some truly horrible things over the course of my career. As a youngster, I was told that if I fainted, cried, or showed any sign of being upset, it would be a sign of weakness, and everyone would laugh at me. I was also told that anything I did would follow me wherever I went and might hold me back from being promoted. The whole atmosphere was toxic and is something that no young person should have to suffer through.

Nowadays, the police service recognizes this and offers counseling and further treatment to anyone who needs it, and there is a full support network set up to help officers deal with things they see and hear while on the job. Long gone are the days of stigma attached to mental health matters, and now we don't have to hide away and deal with things ourselves. Schools have made the same changes, and this is part of the reason why teens today are able to speak up about their own mental health needs. While struggling with your mental health is no longer the norm, there's enough visibility in the media and through school campaigns for teens in trouble to know that they're not alone and won't be ridiculed for reaching out.

**Feeling Great, Mind and Body**

Improving your mental health will not only make you a happier and more relaxed person; it will have far-reaching effects on all aspects of your life. You will have more energy, and you can focus on school work, socializing, forming relationships, and being physically active—all things you need for a fulfilling and rewarding life. You will also find that the things you do are more enjoyable, as you won't be feeling anxious or guilty about your choices.

So, how do you go about fixing your mental health and making sure that you get the best out of every day? There are a number of different things you can try, and we'll have a look at a number of them over the course of this book. From antidepressants to yoga, and meditation to exercise, each treatment is designed to help you manage unhelpful thoughts, calm down after an upsetting situation, or act as a tonic to stop your mental health from slipping. Some of them will have to be prescribed or referred by a medical professional, but there are plenty of others that you can take control of and use at home in a way that is helpful for you. Journaling can help you to analyze your thoughts and see where you could reframe some of your experiences. Talk therapies can give you strategies to get through situations that give you anxiety, like talking to new people or dealing with conflict at home.

You only need a quick search online to see how many books there are that promise to help you understand

and beat depression or anxiety through the use of workbooks, exercises, and other well-worn strategies. But unless you know exactly which method works best for you, it can be confusing where to start. In this book, we're going to examine different mainstream and alternative therapies, give you some examples of the kind of exercises, medication, and activities involved, and let you see for yourself what each treatment entails so that you can make an informed decision about where to go for help. For some of you, dialectical behavioral therapy might be what you need to curb your panic attacks, but others might find that lavender essential oil works just as well.

## An Urgent Need

Cases of teenage mental health disorders are still rising. For all the good that schools, youth workers, and the media are doing to publicize how to get help, there are still a significant number of teenagers who are not getting access to the treatment they need. Some cultures still view mental health as a taboo subject and refuse to acknowledge that their young people need support. Ethnic minorities and teens from poorer households are also less likely to reach out for help, perhaps because there isn't any help to access in their communities, or because they don't feel like therapy is something they can afford or something that is designed to help their situation. For these people, it's even more important that we keep the conversation going.

Your teenage years are such a short part of your life. They shouldn't be the defining factor that the rest of your life is ruled by. Having good mental health now will teach you so much about dealing with stress, anxiety, and depression, that you will be a more resilient and successful adult. This book is designed to introduce you to some of the signs and symptoms of the three most common adolescent mental health disorders so that you can recognize if you need to ask for help. It is also going to introduce you to a wide range of therapies available so that you can go on and research further the ones that will work best for you. Treat the following pages as your one-stop shop for therapy and dive straight into the chapter that you recognize as most relevant, or read straight through to get all the info on how to best look after yourself.

When you're finished, keep it as a reference guide, or pass it on to a friend who you think will benefit from the same advice and information. When you're struggling with low mental health, sometimes the best treatment is recognition and understanding from those you care about. Never underestimate the impact that checking in with your friends can have; you can't always tell who needs to talk and who needs your support.

## YOUR FREE GIFT

As a way of saying thank you for your interest in my work, I'm delighted to offer you a gift that will boost your self-confidence... ***"The Teens' Guide to Overcoming Shyness"***.
Start meaningful conversations with anyone using this guide packed with topics, questions, and tips.
**Pick up your free copy here:**

Teens' Guide to Overcoming Shyness

Click

Teens' Guide to Overcoming Shyness

\*\*\*

**Other books in the *Teens' Guide Series*...**

*TEENS' GUIDE TO MAKING FRIENDS*

***

# TEENS' GUIDE TO HEALTH AND MENTAL WELL...

*TEENS' GUIDE TO DATING*

***

*TEENS' GUIDE TO FINANCIAL INDEPEN-DENCE*

# TEENS' GUIDE TO HEALTH AND MENTAL WELL...

# Chapter One

## What Do We Mean by Mental Health?

*Mental health problems don't define who you are. They are something you experience. You walk in the rain and you feel the rain, but you are not the rain.* –Matt Haig

The term "mental health" seems to be used for almost everything nowadays. Schools and workplaces have mental health first aiders, having bad mental health is now a valid reason to take time off work (I wish it had been when I was younger!), and social media is full of memes about social anxiety and avoiding people. But in all the noise, the explanation of what exactly mental health is seems to have gotten lost. How can you look after something you don't properly understand?

We all know how to be physically healthy, and the results of eating better and exercising more are easily seen. You can tell almost straightaway if your physical health is improving, or if it is declining. Any problems, like an injury or an illness, are also straightforward to diagnose and treat.

Unfortunately, being mentally healthy isn't as straightforward. What keeps one person feeling good, doesn't necessarily work for another, and things that can lower your mental health—like having a bad diet or being isolated—affect people differently too. In the same way that some people are genetically predisposed to physical conditions like diabetes, nearsightedness, and breast cancer, others are more likely to suffer from depression, anxiety, schizophrenia, and other mental health issues.

## A Picture of (Mental) Health

Mental well-being is such a huge topic that it depends on a number of factors. These can be grouped into three different sections: your emotional well-being, social well-being, and psychological well-being. They're all linked together, so if your emotional well-being is suffering, the others will too, and this is part of what makes it so difficult to find the root cause of mental health issues.

## Emotional Well-Being

This takes into account all your feelings and emotions, the way you react to different situations, your ability to deal when things go wrong, and your outlook on life. Having good emotional health doesn't mean that you're happy all of the time, but it does mean that when you have a negative emotion you are able to process it and move forward. It can also give you the strength to make good decisions, like eating a banana instead of a chocolate bar when you're tired because you understand that it will give you more long-lasting energy instead of a sugar rush.

When your emotional well-being is low, it will feel like something bad happening is the end of the world, even if it's something relatively small like getting a stain on your new top or having an argument with your best friend. You will find yourself reacting negatively to change, mistakes, criticism, and disappointment. All of this will also make it harder for you to maintain good relationships with people.

## Social Well-Being

As the name suggests, this aspect of mental health is all about the connections and relationships you have with other people. Humans aren't designed to be alone and we experience a number of benefits from spending time with friends, including lower stress levels, increased confidence, and a more positive mood.

Some people enjoy socializing with large groups of people and have the stamina to handle multiple nights out, deep conversations, and social interactions in the same week. Others would find the same interactions exhausting and overstimulating. These types of people are often referred to as extroverts and introverts, and regardless of how often or how intense they want their social activities to be, both enjoy the same benefits from spending time with the people that they love.

If your social well-being is low, you might find yourself repeatedly canceling plans or turning down invites. Or you might be struggling to make any meaningful connections with people. You will feel isolated and invisible, which can then have a negative effect on your self-worth.

**Psychological Well-Being**

Psychological well-being is shown through your behaviors and perceptions. If this area of your mental health is strong, you will have a positive outlook on life, be able to plan for the future, and see opportunities and possibilities. You will find it easier to treat others kindly and help out when needed, and you'll feel good for doing so. When something bad or unexpected happens, you will be able to see solutions and positive outcomes, even if things initially seem difficult.

If life seems to be always against you, it might be because your psychological well-being is suffering. You're unable to see a positive ending for yourself and can't picture anything good in your future. You'll find it easier to focus on unlucky events and times when things haven't gone your way and be less likely to remember when things have gone well. This can lead to careless and reckless behavior—because you assume the worst is coming anyway—and making a series of short-term decisions rather than considering the bigger picture.

**Mental Health Disorders**

You can have low mental health without having a diagnosable disorder, just like you can have a cough without it being pneumonia, tonsillitis, or a chest infection. However, it's worth highlighting that there are some common mental health conditions that may be underpinning your mental health battle. They aren't always easy to diagnose, though, often relying on you being referred to a specialist and compiling a list of relevant symptoms and behaviors. It's believed that as many as one in seven young people aged 10-19 could be affected by a mental health disorder, but not all of these will be diagnosed and treated (World Health Organization, 2021).

# TEENS' GUIDE TO HEALTH AND MENTAL WELL...

Some of the most common mental health disorders that are diagnosed among teenagers are:

- ADD/ADHD
- anxiety disorders
- bipolar disorder
- eating disorders
- major depressive disorder
- OCD
- schizophrenia

If you suspect that you are affected by any of these disorders, the best thing to do is to make an appointment to speak to your family doctor who will be able to discuss your symptoms, offer treatments, and refer you to a specialist if appropriate.

## The Forces Against You

Predicting how things are going to affect your mental health is pretty much impossible. All your friends and family like different foods, movies, and music, right? There might be some crossovers, but pretty much everyone's combination of tastes is unique, as are their looks, personalities, and their reactions to stressful situations.

You can't tell by looking at your peers whether they're going to stress out over exams, meeting new people, or getting stuck on their homework. There will always be a couple of people who seem to shrug off everything life throws at them, and others who crack at the first obstacle. That's just how your brain is programmed and it's nothing to worry about or be ashamed of if you think you aren't handling things as well as others. Don't forget, it's also very likely that they will be feeling different on the inside than they show on the outside. This generation of teenagers is much better at talking about their mental health than any that went before them, but that doesn't mean everyone is happy with their friends knowing that they're feeling depressed.

There are lots of different events and situations that can wear down your mental health, and the more of these factors people have to face, the more likely it is that they will start to struggle. Some are fairly common and affect pretty much every teen at some stage, whereas others are more traumatic but thankfully rarer.

**Biological**

Not a lot you can do about this one I'm afraid! If there are close relatives in your family who have been diagnosed with mental health disorders, it's likely that you might be more susceptible to developing issues yourself. The way your brain reacts is determined by thousands of genes, and each of these genes carries its own percentage risk for you developing mental health problems. If lots of these genes have a high-risk factor, this adds up and makes it more likely that you might develop mental health problems when faced with some of the other triggers in this section. However, if most of these genes have a low-risk factor, then you are less likely to develop serious mental health issues.

## Environmental

What you're exposed to on a daily basis—at home, at school, and everywhere in between—makes up your environment, and if this is unstable or stressful, this can flood your brain with cortisol. In large quantities, this hormone can disrupt your brain's normal patterns, making it more difficult to sleep and making you feel depressed and anxious.

Increased stress can be caused by not having a secure home life—financial worries, parents splitting up, frequently moving house, or living somewhere unsuitable. These are constant factors, meaning you are always in a state of heightened stress. Other factors might be intermittent, such as experiencing traumatic events, violence, abuse, and bullying, and these can have a profound negative effect on your mental health.

## Social

We all want to feel like we fit in, especially teenagers. The way that your brain rewires itself during puberty means that you become much more socially aware, and with that comes worrying about what other people think of you. When you were a kid you'd probably think nothing of wearing your favorite superhero costume to the park—it made you happy and that was all that mattered. But can you imagine turning up to school now dressed as Spider-Man or Wonder Woman? As a teen, what your peers think of your outfit, your hobbies, your family, and your grades are all as important—sometimes more so—than how you feel about them. That's a lot of pressure on you to always appear "normal," especially if you're feeling low or going through a difficult time.

Peer pressure has become even worse now that social media is everywhere. Scrolling through hundreds of posts of your classmates enjoying themselves can make your life seem dull and empty by comparison. Social media has also brought bullies online and given them another way to put people down and make them feel bad. It's no wonder then that social pressures can really put a dampener on your mental health.

## Academic

# TEENS' GUIDE TO HEALTH AND MENTAL WELL...

No one can be perfect all the time, however much their caregivers want them to be. Teenagers especially are prone to doing stupid things—you can't help it; blame Puberty Brain!—and they don't always have the best work ethic. It might be family that's putting pressure on you to ace your exams and get into a top university, or you might be driven by your own ambition, but either way, those high expectations come with a lot of mental baggage. Anxiety over exams or coursework marks, putting yourself under constant stress to succeed, and feeling depressed if you aren't getting the results you need, can seriously hamper your mental health.

## Hormonal

Even if you live a comfortable life, without academic pressures and plenty of strong friendships, you can still experience mental health issues. During puberty, your body is going through a complete internal reworking and the main reason for this is increased production of either testosterone or estrogen. Everything in your body is run by hormones, and a slight increase or decrease in any one can make you feel completely out of sorts. If you have a menstrual cycle (or live with someone who does), you're probably aware of this by now! Fortunately, most hormonal fluctuations are short-lived, so you might have one day where you feel angry and tired for no reason, and the next you're back to normal. However, if you're taking hormone supplements, it might be a few weeks or months before your body finds its new rhythm.

If you find that you're constantly tired, are gaining weight easily, suffering from frequent headaches, and having problems getting to sleep or feeling refreshed when you wake up, these might be signs that you're suffering from a hormonal imbalance. Most family doctors will be able to order a hormone screening test to see if your levels are within the correct ranges.

## Substances

Alcohol and illegal drugs can mess around with the way that your brain processes chemicals and hormones, increasing the likelihood of you developing mental health problems. Some people use drugs and alcohol to make themselves feel better because they are already in a mental health crisis. I'll explore this more in chapter six, but the important thing to remember is if you use drugs to feel happy, you will find it more difficult to feel happy without them. This is because they overstimulate your brain's happiness receptors, desensitizing them so that smaller feelings of happiness don't register.

## Be Your Own Diagnostician

# TEENS' GUIDE TO HEALTH AND MENTAL WELL...

How easy is it to work out that your mental health might need some attention? One of the reasons why mental health is such a big talking point right now is because spotting the signs that yours is failing is really difficult. Even if you know exactly what you should be looking out for and how you should be feeling, we're generally not very good at evaluating our own well-being. It takes a certain amount of self-awareness to say, "I should be feeling happier than this," and often a mental health crisis (despite the dramatic name) will creep up on you. With the exception of hormonal fluctuations, which can take you from laughing to crying in a matter of minutes, most mood changes happen gradually. You won't wake up in the morning suddenly feeling stressed and anxious, but you might have the realization that you can't remember the last time that you weren't. That's how most people find out that their mental health could do with a tune-up.

So, if you want to be better at evaluating your own mental health, what sort of signs and symptoms should you be looking for?

- feeling sad, hopeless, or depressed for a continuous period of days. Severe depression is classed as a low mood that prevails for at least two weeks, but it's not uncommon for depressive periods to last for a couple of days at a time.

- experiencing frequent mood swings. If you find

yourself easily irritated, angered, or just emotionally sensitive, it could be an indicator of something not being quite right.

- losing interest in hobbies and socializing. Sometimes you just don't have the energy to see people, but if it's happening more often and your social habits are drastically changing, it could be that your mental health is low and you're struggling to cope with the extra stimulation. When you're feeling depressed, you find it harder to get pleasure from things, so you don't get that reward of happiness from activities you used to enjoy. Finding it hard to concentrate on a book, movie, or video game, or no longer enthusiastic about playing your favorite sport? It could be because your levels of serotonin need a boost.

- finding it harder to fall asleep or stay asleep, needing to take naps part way through the day, or waking up still feeling tired. Having low mental health affects your energy and can leave you feeling like an old phone that won't charge properly anymore.

- a change in your relationship with food. Some people comfort eat when they feel down, often craving sweet foods that are high in sugar. Others find it difficult to eat anything and may experience digestive issues like constipation and stomach pain. This can also lead to fluctuations in your weight.

- a noticeable change in grades at school. When you're anxious or stressed about something, it can affect your ability to concentrate and make it difficult for you to finish your work to a good quality. If you're struggling with depression, you may not have the motivation to apply yourself academically, and putting effort into your work will feel too difficult.

## **Get Support**

According to a recent study (Fasihi Harandi et al., 2017), there is a strong relationship between your mental health and the amount of support you receive. People who don't feel they can ask for help, or who don't feel that their wishes will be followed, are far more likely to suffer from mental health issues than people with strong peer and family support networks.

Why are these relationships so valuable? Being able to talk with someone else about your problems can make them seem smaller and less significant. It can also make it easier to spot a solution if there are two or more of you thinking about it. People in your support network can also help you to make changes, like exercising more or eating better, by doing them with you. Forcing yourself to go for a walk when you feel depressed takes a lot of effort, but having a friend turn up and take you out makes the activity seem much more appealing. You get a happy hormone boost from the exercise and from spending time with someone you like—it's a win-win situation!

You might feel that you already have a good support network, in which case you're very lucky. Not everyone has friends or family that they feel they can talk to about mental health issues. If you are looking to find some extra support, here are a few places you could look:

- Teachers and counselors at school are trained to listen to any problems their students come forward with. They will be able to make suggestions to overcome some of your issues and point you in the right direction to get more specialized help if needed.

- A number of charities and organizations offer local or online support groups and forums where you can speak to peers who are going through, or who have been through, some of the same difficulties as yourself. At the back of this book, you will find a list of some international agencies that can help with everything from dealing with alcoholic parents to fighting an eating disorder and overcoming exam stress.

- Talk to friends and family who are far away if you think they can help. Sometimes the people furthest from your current situation can have a more objective view and be able to offer better support. Thanks to modern technology like video calls and cloud gaming, you can relax and enjoy spending time with anyone. Your closest friend doesn't need to be in the room with you to help you feel better.

- Use your local religious center. They run groups and events for people in the community and have volunteers who are always willing to listen to your problems. The leaders can offer you practical and spiritual guidance and they will have lots of experience in helping people through similar situations.

- Your local family doctor will be able to assess your mental health and show you ways to improve it. This could be by starting a course of medication to address a chemical imbalance, by referring you to talk therapy, or pointing you in the direction of some peer support groups. They will have seen lots of teenagers come to talk about their issues, so you needn't be worried that they will think you're weird, weak, or making it up. You probably won't even be the only person they see that day with mental health struggles, so don't worry about telling them exactly how you are feeling.

## Mental Health in Different Cultures

One huge factor that we haven't looked at yet that can contribute to failing mental health is your cultural background. Some cultures take a much more liberal view of mental health, whereas others still feel that it is a taboo subject. Some cultures view taking antidepressants, going to therapy, or being diagnosed with a mental health disorder as a sign of weakness and something that is dishonorable.

This can make it particularly hard to either admit that you are struggling or find someone within your social circle to talk to. Finding resources tailored to your situation, or practitioners who understand your experiences, can be tricky. This doesn't help when you already feel like there's something wrong with you.

Everyone deserves to be healthy, both physically and mentally. Access to good mental health care shouldn't be hampered by stigmas imposed on you by your friends, family, or culture.

## Fight the Statistics

When your mental health is low, you can feel isolated from the people around you. They all look happy and successful, but you feel like you're barely holding it together. The reality couldn't be further from the truth. Actually, it's highly likely that there are several people in your class who are struggling with their own mental health issues. According to a UK study from 2021 (Young Minds, 2021), as many as one out of every six young people under the age of 16 were identified as having a potential mental health disorder. Alarmingly, that amount had increased by nearly 50% in just four years. Even more concerning, around half of 17- to 19-year-olds who had been diagnosed with a mental health disorder admitted to having self-harmed or attempted suicide at some point in their lives.

Mental health is a global concern. In 2020, in the US, one in six young people (aged 12-17) suffered a period of depression lasting longer than two weeks, and 3 million of them reported having suicidal thoughts. Suicide is one of the top three causes of death for children and young adults aged 10-24, and that increases for youth of a racial or gender minority. (National Alliance on Mental Illness, 2023).

You're not alone in your struggles, but if you continue to believe that you are, you're less likely to get help. Never be afraid to reach out to people for the support that you need. Most mental health disorders are easily treatable, and getting help in your teens dramatically reduces the chances of you continuing to struggle as an adult.

# Chapter Two

# Physical Help For Mental Health

*Your mental health is everything – prioritize it. Make the time like your life depends on it, because it does.* –Mel Robbins

One of the best ways that most people can help their mental health is by engaging in regular physical exercise. Even a brisk 10-minute walk can quickly brighten your mood and take your mind off whatever it has been worrying about. Mental health problems can leave you feeling like you don't have any energy, so if the thought of going from crashing out on the sofa to playing football or running 5k fills you with dread, don't worry. There are loads of different ways that you can increase your physical activity to a level that suits you.

Not everyone finds it easy to incorporate activity into their daily routine. You might have physical limitations, be on medication that affects your ability to be active, or suffer from a mental health disorder that makes it difficult for you to cope with making the change. Just because physical activity is suggested for you, doesn't mean that it is right for everyone and in every situation. If you do decide to try being more physically active, make sure you stick to the level of activity that you can cope with and never push yourself to do anything that might be damaging to your health.

## The Ingredients for Mental Wellness

Why is physical exercise so effective in combating low mental health? To understand why, we should first have a look at what exactly goes on in your brain when your mental health is struggling.

## The Cast of Chemicals

Your brain is basically a huge messaging hub, responsible for sending and receiving information to and from the rest of your body. These messages are carried by a network of nerves, but they rely on chemicals called neurotransmitters to create the messages in the first place. These neurotransmitters are read by special receptors that will either be excited and produce happy feelings, or they will be calmed down and make you feel relaxed.

There are three main neurotransmitters that can have a huge effect on how you are feeling and whether your mental health is stable. These are called serotonin, dopamine, and norepinephrine. There are other hormones that can also affect your brain, like cortisol and adrenaline, however. All these neurotransmitters and hormones have a range where they are present in the perfect amount, and when you have too much or too little of one of them, that can affect your mental health. Think of it like making a piece of toast—too much heat and it will burn, not enough and it will be soggy, but there's a stage in the middle that is right for you.

**The Roles They Play**

Serotonin helps your brain to keep everything running smoothly. It tells your brain when you've had enough to eat, when you need to sleep, and generally keeps you in a calm and neutral mood. It can also make you feel happy because you are satisfied. This is a gentle happiness, like when you're enjoying a book you're reading or spending time with loved ones, rather than spikes of excitement or enjoyment. It is a calming chemical, and when its levels are low, it can cause anxiety and depression.

Dopamine is an exciting neurotransmitter. When you have lots of it, it can make you feel excited and even euphoric. It is read by the front part of your brain that deals with rewards. When you do something you enjoy, you get rewarded with a hit of dopamine. This makes you want to do it again. Low levels of dopamine can make you feel sluggish and lacking in energy. You also might not feel happy as a reward for doing something you usually enjoy, which can contribute to a low mood.

Norepinephrine is a neurotransmitter and a hormone that tells your brain when you should be feeling stressed. You might already know that adrenaline is released when you feel stressed, triggering what is known as a fight or flight response: Your body gets a burst of energy to use to either run away from something scary or fight back. Low levels of norepinephrine can also cause depression, but high levels can leave you feeling anxious and stressed out.

## A Balancing Act

When the levels of some or all of these neurotransmitters are out of normal range, your brain finds it difficult to function as normal. This affects the way you feel, the way you react to different situations, your energy levels, and your emotions. Chemical imbalances are found in the brains of people diagnosed with mental health disorders like depression, schizophrenia, and bipolar disorder.

Chemical imbalances can be treated with antidepressants. They usually work by helping your brain receptors to absorb higher levels of serotonin and norepinephrine. Often, feeling depressed and lethargic stops people from being able to deal with the cause of their problems, so antidepressants can be a useful way to make yourself feel well enough for talk therapies or other treatments to be effective.

## Why Exercise Makes You Feel Good

Exercise increases the production and absorption of dopamine. This lights up the reward centers of your brain and gives you instant feel-good feedback. Strenuous exercise is particularly good for this, and that means anything that raises your heart rate, even if it's just for a short period of time. Sometimes all it takes to immediately feel happier is to dance to your favorite song. Once your mood has been lifted, you will probably feel less overwhelmed by your problems and be able to think more clearly about things you want or need to do.

Different kinds of exercise will have different results for your brain. High-intensity exercise will make you feel great, but gentler exercise can make you feel relaxed, less stressed, and help to clear your mind of troubling thoughts. But everything, when performed regularly, will help your brain to lower the levels of stress hormones (cortisol and adrenaline) in your body. This will also make it easier for you to sleep, restoring your energy levels.

If you exercise with a friend or decide to take up a team sport, you will also have the added bonus of increasing your social well-being. Regular interactions with other people promote the production of serotonin and dopamine, making you feel happy and fulfilled. Socializing with others will also encourage your brain to release hormones called endorphins that reduce cortisol levels and make you feel less stressed.

## A Weighty Issue

So far I've been focusing on how physical and mental health are linked by talking about how exercise can make you feel better. You might be wondering if it works the other way too—does feeling depressed have a bad effect on your physical health?—and, unfortunately, the answer is yes.

If your mental health is suffering, you lose the motivation to do things that you enjoy or that are good for you. This can include exercising and eating healthy foods. If this happens, most of us will start to gain weight, and if that's an unwanted side effect, it's something else for you to feel down about.

Being overweight or underweight can be a huge source of stress, especially during your teenage years. Your bodies are changing shape, and putting on weight is a natural part of this. However, some of these changes can leave you feeling self-conscious and with low self-esteem, especially when you start to compare yourself to peers or celebrities. There are a lot of images and articles floating around the internet that talk about ideal weights, body shapes, and what your BMI should be, which unintentionally heap on the pressure to be "normal." What these things don't take into account is your culture, race, fitness level, height, diet, genetic makeup, and just about every other defining feature that makes you who you are.

Some people are not going to be supermodel thin, no matter how fit they are, and some people are never going to have curves, no matter how much they eat. That's just how it is, I'm afraid. Does being overweight or underweight mean you're not healthy or fit? Not necessarily, because your fitness levels and your weight levels aren't as closely related as you think. Your weight is decided by your metabolism and where your body decides to build its fat stores. You can absolutely have curves and muscles that give you a high BMI, but still be capable of running 10K or playing a high-tempo sport. Look at any American Footballer: No one would deny that they are incredible athletes, yet quite a few of them have a large build that has nothing to do with muscle mass. Then there are performers like Beyonce and Lizzo, who pull off energetic performances night after night when on tour, and neither is built like a stereotypical dancer.

## Healthy Fitness Levels

Instead of focusing on trying to achieve a perfect weight—something that can increase your levels of stress and depression, especially if you are quite a lot larger than your target—you could instead focus on reaching an acceptable level of fitness. Not only is this easy to do, regardless of your body type, but it will also make you healthier, both physically and mentally. Unless you have a medical condition that limits your movement, the following is a starting point for activities you should be able to do without difficulty:

- Climb a flight of stairs without getting out of breath. Your heart rate and your breathing rate should stay pretty much the same at the top of the stairs as they were at the bottom, provided you walk up at your normal speed.

- Bend over, touch your toes, and stand up again. This exercise uses your core muscles—the muscles in your stomach and back—that keep you upright and help you to balance.

- Stand up from lying or sitting on the floor without pulling yourself up on furniture or using other people to help you. Again, this uses your core muscles, as well as your legs and arms.

- Be able to unpack two full bags of groceries without getting out of breath. As well as being a test of whether you can do something mildly active for at least five minutes, it will test your range of motion, because you'll be bending and reaching into different cupboards and different heights.

If you find any of these activities difficult, it might indicate that you need to improve your fitness or your muscle tones.

## The Energy Cycle

You might think that exercising more will make you feel tired, but exercising actually has the opposite effect: It gives you more energy than you started with! This is because the endorphins that are produced by exercise reward you for moving by giving you a boost of energy and lifting your mood. Increased endorphin levels can also improve the quality of your sleep, helping you rest better and, therefore, feel more refreshed in the morning. So, if you find it hard to find the energy or motivation to do anything, it could be a sign that you're not active enough. Once you start increasing your activity levels, you should see an improvement in your energy levels to match.

## How to Start Exercising

Knowing that you need to get more exercise is one thing, but actually getting started can be much harder, especially if you're trying something that you've not done before. How do you know what kind of exercise will be right for you? Will you enjoy it? Is it something that a beginner will find easy to get into? You might try a couple of things that aren't a good fit, but don't be disheartened, it's perfectly normal not to find your perfect activity straightaway. It's a bit like dating. Very rarely does your first relationship end up being your soulmate. I remember being excited when my school started offering golf as a sport—it was so different to everything else and I couldn't wait to have a go. Unfortunately, my first shot sent the ball sailing straight through the woodwork classroom window, and it was strongly suggested that I stick to running instead!

Luckily, because being physically healthy has been in the public consciousness for decades, there are hundreds of sports classes, online tutorials, apps, and books aimed at inspiring you and getting you moving. No matter your existing fitness level or your past experiences with sports, you will be able to find an enjoyable and effective way of increasing your activity.

## If You Want to Start Immediately

The easiest form of exercising is walking or running. You don't need any specialist equipment; you can start from your front door, and there are no techniques, rules, or methods to learn. You can also simply measure your progress by timing how long it takes you to walk somewhere, or how far you can get in a set time.

Start by setting yourself a short route in a familiar area. This could be around the block, to a friend's house, or exploring a local park. If you want to track your sessions, you can download apps that will plot your route on a map, count your steps, and even estimate your walking speed.

As your fitness increases, you can find longer walks and add in some sections with hills to give your leg muscles and your heart an extra workout. Other ways to build up your sessions include:

- alternating between walking, running, and sprinting for different distances

- adding stretches at regular intervals to improve flexibility

- stopping every ten minutes to do one minute of exercises like jumping jacks, sit-ups, or high kicks, to get your heart pumping

## If You Want to Teach Yourself

The internet is a treasure trove of resources to get people into exercise. YouTube has many videos of everything from aerobics to Zumba, or dance lessons to yoga. You can even learn how to sail, paddleboard, or ice skate if you fancy trying something a bit more quirky. The best part? You can watch a couple of videos before deciding to try anything for yourself.

When looking for a good instructional video, make sure you choose one that is for beginners or one with an instructor who explains how to accomplish poses or moves at different levels. Often yoga or pilates teachers will demonstrate several adaptations of a pose to make them accessible to everyone. Once you find something you like, check to see if there are other videos that progress, so that you can build on your workout. Some YouTube channels offer select videos for free, but then ask you to subscribe if you want to see the rest. It's up to you whether you can afford this, or whether you just want to stick with the free workouts.

Clear a big enough space to exercise in so that you aren't at risk of tripping over a rug or knocking something

# TEENS' GUIDE TO HEALTH AND MENTAL WELL...

valuable off a bookshelf. Set up your video to play on the TV, tablet, phone, or computer somewhere you can easily see what you should be copying. Never overstretch yourself—if it starts to hurt, or you feel strong resistance, stop.

## If You Need Encouragement

Some apps offer forums and support groups to their members, as well as set fitness plans and workouts that are designed to tone specific parts of your body. There is often a subscription or purchase fee, but it's usually less than a gym membership. Alternatively, you could try encouraging friends to support you by joining you on your walks, swimming together, or signing up for the same spin classes.

Other apps or online programs, like Couch to 5K, set you a series of achievable milestones to encourage you on your fitness journey. By slowly increasing the amount of time you exercise, you'll soon see your stamina increase. You could also encourage yourself by setting motivational targets with specific rewards when you complete them. Some good targets include: the first time you run 1 kilometer, being able to hold a tricky yoga pose for ten seconds, or just managing a seven-day exercise streak.

## If You Want to Exercise Alone

Walking, running, and swimming are all great ways of getting fit by yourself while also giving you time to improve your mental health wellness. While exercising, you can focus on clearing your head of all those annoying random thoughts that build up over the day. These are so much easier to sort through and clear out when you're doing a simple, repetitive activity, like swimming laps of a pool. When you're walking or running, you can pop some headphones in so that the world doesn't distract you—this won't work while you're swimming though, even with earbuds, as water and electricity definitely don't mix!

On the subject of swimming, you can add in extra activities to your sessions, just like you can to your runs. Find yourself a quiet spot outside of the swimming lanes and add in some stretches, squats, and balances in between your lengths. If you enjoy exercising in the water but want to try something different, you could see if your pool offers aqua fitness classes—this is like aerobics but in the water, which increases the resistance against your muscles and makes them work a little bit harder.

## If You Want Company

Your local gym will run a schedule of classes over the week that lets new people join at any time. You might also find some places running courses over a number of weeks. These are often aimed at beginners who feel a little apprehensive about jumping straight into a class with more experienced people. You can go to classes by yourself or take a friend with you. Why not take it in turn with your friends to pick something new to learn? One month you could all be learning Latin dancing; the next week it could be kickboxing.

Exercising as a group builds your physical wellness and your social wellness. It's a great way to meet new people who like some of the same things as you. Your school will have a number of different sports teams you could try out for, but there will also be community sports groups that are always looking for new people to join. Sports like basketball, netball, football, hockey, and water polo tick all the boxes for being fun, active, and social.

Martial arts classes are another popular way to get fit, build your confidence, and learn some useful self-defense skills. Karate, judo, and kickboxing are high-energy sports that will build your strength and stamina, while Tai Chi is a more meditative and calming class that uses gentle, fluid movements to keep your joints supple and help you improve your balance and core strength.

## Yoga for Mental Health

To get you started on your journey to better physical and mental health, I wanted to include a few simple yoga routines. Yoga is a great way to exercise—it can be done on your own or in groups, and the exercises are simple, but you can build on them by joining several into a sequence or changing the intensity of the stretch. Yoga builds up your muscles and strengthens your core, but it also increases your flexibility and the range of movement you are capable of. It doesn't raise your heart rate like cardio or HIIT, instead, it relaxes you and helps you to empty your mind by using breathing techniques and visualizations.

Each of these routines is designed to last five minutes, but you can combine them or repeat them if you want to work out for longer.

## A Morning Routine to Wake You Up

This sequence is designed to get your positive energy flowing and gently stretch and loosen your muscles after a night in bed.

Start in **mountain pose**: Stand with your feet together and stretch your arms above your head. Bring your palms together and lean into a gentle back bend while exhaling, only going as far as you are able.

Take a deep breath and exhale as you bend your knees and sit backward as if there is a chair there—exactly why this is called **chair pose**! Keep your arms extended above your head. Get as low as you can, but don't bend your knees or waist beyond a right angle. Try and hold this pose for thirty seconds, but stand up sooner if you experience any pain. Take a deep breath and exhale as you stand back up.

You're now going to go into a **forward fold**. Take a deep breath in and, as you exhale, lengthen your spine and bend from the waist so that you fold forward. Bring your arms out to the side as you go. Hold that hanging position for three breaths, with your head and arms just dangling.

Place your hands on the floor (you may need to bend your knees slightly to do this). Walk your palms forward into **downward-facing dog**. Your weight should be equally distributed between your feet and hands, so lean back into your hips and keep your spine straight. Push the weight down through your heels, getting them as low to the ground as you can.

Bring one knee into your chest and step through your hands into a **forward lunge position,** placing your foot on the floor and dropping your other knee. You can either rest it on the floor or hover just above it for a deeper stretch. Raise your arms up above your head and hold for one breath, then bring them back down and step your front leg back into downward-facing dog. Repeat for the other leg.

## A Routine to Energize You

Stand in the **mountain pose** with your feet together and your arms by your side. Now move into **Warrior I**: Step your left foot back and bend your right knee, so that you're in a lunging position. You can choose how far back to step to make sure that you don't overstretch yourself. Turn your left foot out by about 45 degrees to help you balance. Sink down into your hips, stretch your arms above your head, and dip into a gentle back bend. Breathe in this position for five seconds.

Turn your left foot out to 90 degrees and rotate your hips to follow it. Instead of facing forward your torso should now be sideways. Drop your arms to the side but keep them at shoulder height. Your right arm should be over your right knee and your left arm over your left leg. Look along your right arm and breathe in this position for five seconds. This is **Warrior II**.

Turn your hands so the palms are facing upward. Lean back until your left hand reaches your left leg and let it slide down as far as you feel comfortable. As you lean back, your right arm should naturally go up; curve it slightly over your head as you move into the **peaceful warrior**.

Straighten both your knees but keep your legs apart. If this stretch is too wide for you, you can readjust and bring your legs closer together. Turn your feet out so your toes are pointing away from each other. Make sure you are facing sideways and your weight is equally balanced between each leg. Bring your palms together in front of your chest with fingertips pointing upward. Gently bend your knees and sink down into **goddess pose**, only going as low as you are comfortable. Breathe in this position for five seconds and then straighten your knees; bring your legs together, and return to mountain pose.

Repeat the entire sequence on the other leg.

## A Relaxing Routine to Help You Unwind

Start by lying on your back with your legs slightly apart and your arms palms up. This is called **savasana** or **corpse pose** and it's a great way to relax and unwind. Breathe slowly and when you exhale, imagine the air leaving your body and washing over you all the way to your feet.

Bring your knees up and place your feet flat on the floor just behind your buttocks. Gently tilt your pelvis forward and backward while keeping your legs, buttocks, and back in place. This helps to release any tension at the base of your spine. Settle your pelvis in a neutral position where it feels comfortable—not tilted too far either way.

Bring your arms into your side, and with your palms facing down, inhale and slowly lift your hips off the floor. Try to imagine your spine rolling up one vertebra at a time as you come into **bridge pose**. Your feet, arms, and shoulders are now on the floor, but your back should be curved away from it. Exhale as you lower yourself back to the starting position, one vertebra at a time. Repeat four more times.

Pull your knees into your chest so that you are curled up into a ball. Bring your arms up the outside of your legs and hold onto your feet or ankles. Stretch your legs away from your body into the **happy baby pose**. You can rock gently from side to side to release any remaining tension in your back.

Roll over so that you are on your hands and knees in a **cat/cow pose**. Keep your back flat and let your head hang down. Breathe in and lift your head up while curving your spine toward the floor. Breathe out and drop your head again, this time arching your back away from the floor. Repeat each pair of movements four more times.

Sink back into **child pose**. Your knees can be either tucked under your stomach or on each side of your torso. Your arms should be stretched forward on the floor, elongating your spine. Rest your forehead on the floor between your elbows. Relax and breathe in this position for one minute.

# TEENS' GUIDE TO HEALTH AND MENTAL WELL...

# Chapter Three

## Overcoming Anxiety

*You don't have to control your thoughts. You just have to stop letting them control you.* –Dan Millman

Over the next three chapters, I'm going to be introducing you to the top three mental health concerns among teenagers today. These are diagnosable disorders in their own right, but also present as symptoms of other conditions—like bipolar disorder and OCD. It's incredibly likely that you will experience at least one of these during your teenage years. In fact, it's perfectly healthy to feel small amounts of stress and anxiety; they're your body's natural response to scary situations, like being trapped in a room with a bear, getting into an argument with a bully, or having to do a class presentation.

# TEENS' GUIDE TO HEALTH AND MENTAL WELL...

A recent study (BBFC, 2021) shows that anxiety is top on the list of mental health issues as far as today's teenagers are concerned, with 50% of respondents listing it as their biggest worry. It's overtaken stress and depression, the other two big names on our list, but why? In this chapter, we'll delve into what anxiety is, how it feels, why so many teens suffer from it, and how you can treat it.

## What Anxiety Feels Like

It's thought that as many as one in three teenagers suffer from anxiety (McCarthy, 2019), with figures being similar in both the UK and the US. There are a number of different anxiety disorders that manifest themselves in slightly different ways. Unlike stress, which is your body's response to a specific situation, anxiety is best described as a feeling of dread or fear, often with no immediately obvious cause. Sometimes this can be specific to situations that involve socializing or linked to worries about your health or appearance. Anxiety can also manifest as panic attacks, and if you've not had one before, they can be frightening.

Different people will experience slightly different symptoms, and these can also change depending on what type of anxiety disorder you are diagnosed with, but some of the main physical symptoms of anxiety include:

- feeling lightheaded or dizzy

- heart palpitations (where your heart rate becomes irregular—speeds up or slows down—without you doing anything to cause it)

- sweating

- feeling like you might be sick

- needing to urinate more often

- a fluttering or churning sensation in your stomach

As you'd expect with a mental health disorder, anxiety doesn't just have physical symptoms; it can mess with your mind too. So, not only might you feel a little wobbly on the outside, but your brain could also be going through some of these mental symptoms:

- not being able to relax or stop worrying

- feeling like everyone is watching you

- feeling disconnected from your body, like you're floating

- thinking about bad things happening to you in the future

- remembering bad things from your past, over and over again

- finding it difficult to enjoy things because it means you might stop worrying

## Generation A (is for Anxiety)

Cases of anxiety in teenagers are rising pretty quickly and studies show that this generation is the most anxious yet (McCarthy, 2022). You're probably sick of hearing the adults in your life telling you that things were so different when they were young, but the world has definitely changed a lot in a pretty short space of time, as we're still working out how to live with those changes. Some of them have undeniably been for the better, but others seem to be having more of a negative effect than was intended.

## Entertainment Overload

Once upon a time, there was only live television. You had to wait until your program was broadcast to be able to watch it, and then wait a week for the next episode. This taught people patience and restraint, as well as how to occupy themselves for short periods of time while they waited for something they wanted.

Now we have a dozen streaming services offering instant entertainment to fill every free minute of your time. Social media reels and videos don't even engage your brain while you watch them—there's no plot to follow, dialogue to digest, or characters to become attached to. On the odd occasion that you're waiting for something live to start, like a sports match, you probably just pick up your phone and scroll the internet to fill the time.

No one feels bored anymore. No one feels frustrated that they can't watch the next episode or sad that they have to wait for it. But, news flash, I'm afraid these feelings didn't just get eradicated. So, when you are forced to be bored, frustrated, or sad, you don't have years of resilience built up, or any coping strategies that really work. That can leave you feeling anxious and out of control.

## The Happiness Plague

On the subject of emotions, it's not just the negative ones that cause problems—sometimes the pressure to feel happy can be unbearable. There's no way you can feel happy all of the time, especially when you're a teen who isn't in control of your feelings, but there's been a recent shift in our culture toward toxic positivity, which tells you that if you aren't happy, there must be something wrong with you. After all, you probably have a family, a home, your own possessions, food to eat, and access to education—all things you should be grateful for, and therefore, happy about.

However, family sometimes annoys us, home can feel claustrophobic, and school isn't always fun. There are going to be occasions when you're not happy with things in your life, and that's okay. But you're made to feel so guilty every time you feel something other than happy, that these negative emotions also end up making you feel anxious that something is wrong with you.

**Antisocial Media**

When social media first started to catch on, it was all about connecting with people, sharing your interests, and staying in touch with family and friends who lived far away. Now it's become a way to show off what you have and what you're doing, and it encourages you to copy others rather than stand out from the crowd. How many TikTok dance videos are original routines and how many are other people copying the trend? How many times do I have to watch Bill Hader dancing to Makeba but with a different background each time?

Social media gives you anxiety because it plays on your need to be accepted. You make a reel, post a photo, or share a meme, and wait for the likes to roll in. Why are other versions of your dance, posted by other people, getting more likes? Why didn't your friend like a photo of your outfit? Why hasn't your friend request been accepted yet?

There's also the constant comparisons with celebrities and exposure to lifestyles that are supposedly better than yours. Being bombarded with images of things you'll never have, while also being told that you should want them, is just going to leave you feeling constantly unfulfilled and unsatisfied.

**The Future Looks Bleak**

Some anxieties are justified, but they can become a problem if you're worrying about them all of the time. There's been so much in the news about climate change and the worsening state of the planet, that it's perfectly understandable if you're a little anxious about what the world might look like when you're older. The same can be said for worrying about getting a job, being able to buy a house, or even just making it through high school without a school shooting on your turf.

**The Pressure to Succeed**

Grown-ups know that competition for jobs and good salaries is fierce, so they probably spend a lot of time telling you how important it is to get really good grades in school. You'll hear this from your family, from your teachers, from celebrities, and from influencers, but you're probably already trying your best anyway. Some of you are also dealing with cultural expectations to study for long hours, take extra subjects, or learn extracurricular skills like musical instruments or languages. That's a lot of people making you feel that you're not doing well enough and putting pressure on you to do even better.

Studying every spare minute you have is going to lead to burnout, where you just don't have the energy or the focus to continue and the thought of doing so makes you feel stressed and anxious. But resting when you know you have work to do also makes you feel anxious—it's impossible to win!

That's a pretty big list of anxiety triggers, but it still only covers the general causes that might affect the majority of teens. You will have things going on in your life that are anxiety triggers specific to you and your situation.

## Easy Come, Easy Go

The good news is that anxiety is pretty easy to manage. There are lots of treatments available and the internet is full of free resources to help you get started while you wait for a referral to go through, or for medication to kick in. I've included some of them at the end of this book in the "Resources" section. Because anxiety is such a common problem, doctors will be used to patients making appointments and asking for help, so you needn't worry that they will judge you or think you're weird.

## Medication

One of the most common treatment options for anxiety is prescription medication. There are a couple of different types that might be offered by your doctor:

- Beta-blockers: These stop your body from producing adrenaline or norepinephrine—two chemicals that can raise your blood pressure and make your heart beat faster. They don't treat the psychological symptoms of anxiety, but they can stop the physical ones. This means that you won't get that panicky feeling of a fluttery stomach and tight chest. When I was younger, I took beta-blockers to help me feel calmer when I was struggling with the pressure of my exams.

- Antidepressants: There are different types of antidepressants, but all of them work by helping your brain balance the chemicals that make you feel happy or sad. This means they treat the psychological symptoms of anxiety as well as the physical ones. They usually take a couple of weeks to build up in your body, so you won't feel better immediately, and you can sometimes feel more anxious while they're starting to work. If you don't feel better after a couple of months you should speak to your doctor about trying a different type.

- Tranquilizers: If your anxiety is so severe that it is stopping you from living your life and you are having frequent panic attacks, your doctor might decide to prescribe you a short course of tranquilizers. They work by slowing down your brain function (so that you stop overthinking and worrying) and making you feel sleepy and relaxed. They can be addictive, which is why you will only be given them for a short period of time, but they are like an emergency stop when your anxiety is running wild.

All of these medications help to relieve the symptoms of your anxiety, but they won't be able to do anything about the causes. However, they are really useful for helping you to feel well enough to start tackling those anxiety triggers, either by yourself or with the help of a therapist. Some people take anxiety medication for a long time, while others just use it for a couple of months because it helps them to feel better and gives them a chance to get over their anxiety, especially if it was caused by a specific trigger like exams or moving house.

**Talk Therapies**

There can still be a bit of a negative stigma around going to see a therapist, but the truth is that we could all use a little help to see through our problems. Sometimes talking to your friends or family members is enough to help you see the next steps, but sometimes you need guidance from a professional with more experience.

- Cognitive Behavior Therapy (CBT): You and your therapist will work together to look at some of the reasons why you think, feel, and act the way you do. You will learn to rewrite some of your behaviors to avoid going into a negative spiral. You and your therapist will talk about what has happened to you during the week and how you coped with situations that made you anxious. They will help you to see where you could have made better choices and give you some activities to practice at home before your next session.

- Mindfulness: This is a type of therapy that focuses on improving your awareness of what is going on around you and how that makes you feel. This will help you notice when you start to feel anxious and then teach you some steps to stop the feelings from growing out of control. This can include making yourself more aware of physical sensations around you in order to take your concentration away from negative thoughts.

- Relaxation Therapies: Your therapist will teach you how to overcome the physical sensations of anxiety through meditation and muscle relaxation techniques. You can then apply these outside of your sessions when you start to feel anxious. It's less of a talk therapy than the others because it doesn't try to change your behavior; however, I've included it here because lots of teens can feel self-conscious talking about their thoughts and feelings, so learning relaxation techniques can feel more accessible.

**Self-Help**

Asking for help can be daunting, especially if you're already feeling anxious! There are some things that you can start doing by yourself that will make you feel better if you're not ready to talk to a professional yet. Actually, a lot of professionals will probably recommend these activities anyway, either as part of talk therapy or alongside taking medication.

- Online CBT Courses: You can follow a set program of exercises designed to help you understand where your anxiety comes from and how to regain control of it. These won't be tailored specifically to you, but they will give you some of the same exercises as a personal therapist would. Some are free and some you will have to pay for, but you can work through them in your own time and at your own pace.

- Workbooks: There are loads of CBT and DBT workbooks available to purchase that will give you practical exercises to do and to analyze your feelings. Some are aimed specifically at teenagers and others are more general.

These activities are designed to help you find and work around the causes of anxiety. Once you have done this, your anxiety won't be triggered (or won't be as bad) in those situations. However, they won't treat the symptoms, so you might not start to feel better for a while. This is why people often pair a course of medication with either self-help methods or talk therapies. The medication suppresses the symptoms of anxiety that make you feel worried and sad, and the exercises help you to root out the cause, so you won't be made to feel that way in the future.

**Anxiety First Aid**

Some situations might make your anxiety worse. For example, if you need to speak to a teacher or you've arranged to go on a date. This can cause your physical symptoms to suddenly get worse or even cause a panic attack. The physical symptoms of anxiety can be very unpleasant, and often, people try and avoid situations, not because they are really dangerous or scary, but because

# TEENS' GUIDE TO HEALTH AND MENTAL WELL...

they don't want to start sweating, blushing, or feeling dizzy.

If your anxiety does start to feel overwhelming, here are some ways you can feel better quickly. It's worth practicing them at home rather than trying them for the first time when you're already feeling anxious. That way, you will feel more prepared for the situation because you know that you have some secret weapons in your mental health arsenal!

- You can slow a fast heart rate by making sure your breathing is slow and regular. Your breathing often speeds up when you feel anxious or start to panic, which makes you feel light-headed because not as much oxygen is getting to your brain. Breathe in through your nose for a count of four, hold it for one, and then breathe out through your mouth for another count of four. If four beats is too long, start with three, and as your breathing becomes more regular, you can make the breaths longer.

- Essential oils like lavender, sandalwood, and chamomile can have a calming effect on your brain. You can buy them in sprays or as little roll-ons that you can discreetly apply to your wrist. When you start to feel anxious, just bring your hand up to your face and take a deep breath, inhaling the scent of the oil. Many people say that smelling the right essential oil can help them to relax, although there is very little scientific research to prove how they affect you.

- If you find that your anxiety makes your brain start thinking of all the things that could go wrong or be bad for you, then you might find a grounding technique called the 333 Method helps you. Grounding aims to remind your brain what is real and what it is imagining, and it helps you focus on your immediate surroundings rather than a set of imagined problems. The 333 Method asks you to name—out loud—three things that you can see, three sounds that you can hear, and three things you can touch. This uses different senses to pull your brain back to reality.

For most people, anxiety builds up slowly, getting a little bit worse overtime, so you probably didn't even notice it happening until it began to stop you from doing things. Even if you think that you can cope with your current anxiety levels, there is no need to because there are so many treatments and coping mechanisms available. You might be surprised by how much better you feel with just a few small changes.

# TEENS' GUIDE TO HEALTH AND MENTAL WELL...

# Chapter Four

## Handling Stress

*You don't have to be positive all the time. It's perfectly okay to feel sad, angry, annoyed, frustrated, scared and anxious. Having feelings doesn't make you a negative person. It makes you human.* –Lori Deschene

Believe it or not, stress can be really useful. It's often the extra push you need to get through a difficult situation, like meeting an essay deadline or asking that special someone out on a date. This energy boost is due to your body releasing a number of stress hormones including adrenaline, norepinephrine, and cortisol. These hormones send signals to your brain to put your body into a special state called "fight or flight" mode: This basically prepares you to either run from what is stressing you out, or fight it. It all goes back to the days when we lived in caves and life was full of scary things that could kill you—now the only things you have to run from are class presentations or unflattering Instagram photos.

Here's an example of what's supposed to happen when you enter a stressful situation:

Ben has a chemistry exam in half an hour and as he waits in another classroom, he begins to worry that he won't do well. This triggers a stress response and his body releases a flood of stress hormones into his bloodstream. Ben's heart begins to beat faster, pumping blood around his body more quickly. His breathing rate also increases, providing more oxygen to his lungs, and his blood vessels get wider so the blood can move around his body more easily. This all ensures that his muscles and organs get a good supply of oxygen and sugar that prepares them for extra activity. During the exam, Ben finds that he is able to think clearly about the questions on the paper because his brain is properly fueled. He finishes the exam and feels pretty good about it. The stress hormones in his body have done their job so his brain sends signals to his glands to stop producing them. Over a period of a few hours, Ben's hormone levels return to normal and he no longer feels stressed. He now feels a bit of a slump in his energy levels and decides to spend the evening watching Netflix with his cat.

## A Helpful Mechanism Backfires

Sometimes, those stress hormone levels don't go back to normal. There can be a number of reasons for this—the stressful situation is ongoing, you experience a number of stressful incidents in a short period of time, or you have an illness affecting your hormone levels—and this is when something that is meant to help you can end up making you feel awful.

When you feel stressed, it can magnify other problems in your life. You could probably handle a pop quiz in history on a normal day, but when you're stressed because you had an argument with your best friend, that pop quiz could seem like the end of the world. A surprise like that could make you panic, react angrily, burst into tears, feel sick, or start shaking. The list of unpleasant symptoms of stress is quite long and everyone reacts differently.

It's not just the ways that teens react to stress that are different; it's the situations that cause this that are different for everyone too. You've probably already noticed that some people seem to take unexpected changes in their stride while others can have their whole day ruined by something not going to plan.

However, when you're already feeling stressed out about something, seeing other people handle the same situation smoothly doesn't do much to make you feel better. Next time you do feel stressed about something, try not to compare yourself to others. Keep the focus on you and what you can do in the situation and don't worry about whether people can see you're stressed and what they will think—the chances are, unless you faint, vomit, or scream, they probably won't even notice.

Anything can cause you stress; you don't need to justify why or try and brush it off because you think it's silly. It's universally acknowledged that exams are stressful, so you often get support to manage how you feel in this situation, and teens find it easier to talk about exam stress because it's a feeling that is shared by many of their peers. Other big changes, like ending a relationship, your parents getting divorced, a death in the family, or learning to drive also seem to be acceptable reasons to feel stressed, according to society.

But what if the cause of your stress is something more niche? It's difficult to talk about because it isn't a group experience. You might be worried that people will laugh at you for being stressed out by something that they don't find a problem. Maybe your neighbor bought a dog and it scares you—now walking past their house every day causes you stress. Or perhaps the day of your tennis lesson got changed to the same day as your swimming club—now you have one day when you're really tired and it's too much.

## When Stress is in Control

Dealing with stress is something that both adults and teenagers have to do, but they both do it in slightly different ways. Because most of the activity in a teenage brain happens in the emotional centers, you can feel the mental effects of stress more strongly, and this can mean your decision-making becomes less reliable. You are also more likely to have a more intense reaction to feeling stressed because your body releases a greater amount of cortisol than an adult's (ReachOut, 2015).

Feeling stressed as a teenager can also have an effect on your mental health as an adult. Your brain goes through a lot of changes during puberty, and stress hormones like cortisol can affect how your brain develops. Studies show that if cortisol levels are high when the stress receptors in your brain are maturing, they can make you more likely to suffer from mental health disorders as an adult. (Romeo, 2013).

I've already talked about the changes you'll feel when your stress hormones are at work, but a racing heart and faster breathing aren't the only signs that something is bothering you. Lots of these symptoms are shared with other mental health disorders like anxiety and depression, so before your doctor settles on a diagnosis, they will probably ask you lots of questions about your lifestyle in general and some of the situations where you feel most stressed out.

# TEENS' GUIDE TO HEALTH AND MENTAL WELL...

## Signs of Stress in Teenagers

- finding it difficult to fall asleep, stay asleep, or waking up in the morning feeling as if you haven't slept

- feeling fatigued all day long

- not feeling hungry

- feeling nauseous

- digestive issues such as being bloated, constipated, or having diarrhea

- headaches that don't seem to be helped by taking painkillers

- feeling irritable, snappy, and angry

- not being able to concentrate on anything, whether it's schoolwork, a conversation, or a hobby

- not wanting to see friends, leave the house, or spend time with family

- feeling sad or depressed

- feeling anxious or panicky

- eating more or less than normal

- not wanting to go to school or partake in lessons

- drinking alcohol (more than usual)

- taking illegal drugs (more than usual)

- erratic behavior that seems dangerous or out of character

I know that's a long list, and some of the items on there—like feeling sleepy all the time or not wanting to go to school—can be a normal part of teenage life. So, how do you know whether you're stressed or just going through a growth spurt, puberty, or a hormonal phase?

I wish there was an easy answer. You can be stressed and have only one of these symptoms, or you can have half a dozen. You need to look at the wider picture: Are there changes happening in your life that could cause stress, or are some of these symptoms lasting for a week or longer? Going through puberty is a stressful time anyway because there are so many changes happening in your body that you can't control. This can make you feel overwhelmed and confused.

Other changes and situations that can make some teenagers feel stressed are:

- starting a new school, moving classes, and having to choose subjects to study

- feeling the need to do well, suddenly struggling in a subject where you have done well before, or an increase in academic expectations from school and home

- exams, feeling underprepared, or overpreparing

- changing relationships with friends or breaking up with a partner

- feeling overwhelmed, having too much to do, or not having enough time to do everything you enjoy

- joining a new club or starting a new sport

- strained relationships at home, divorce or separation, or a death in the family

- moving house or having a sibling or parent move out

## Stick to the Plan

Some things, like schoolwork or friendship issues, will become less stressful when you become an adult, but growing up brings new stresses of its own. If you learn to deal with stressful situations when you are a teenager, you will find it easier to handle feeling stressed out as an adult. Unless you win the lotto, move to a deserted island, and pay people to deal with your problems for you, you're always going to have to navigate some sort of stress. Avoiding it is just impractical. So, what can you do to help calm yourself down when you find yourself getting stressed out with day-to-day life?

Get yourself a daily or weekly planner. I know you can do them online or on your phone, but you'll be surprised how much it helps writing everything out and being able to see it all laid out in advance. Add all your classes, clubs, activities, and shifts at work, as well as any other things you do regularly and can't miss, like going to church or eating dinner as a family. Now look at all the blank spaces. This is your time for writing assignments, studying for tests, seeing friends, and relaxing. I bet it's more than you thought you'd have.

Look at the assignments, class reading, and revision that you need to do for the upcoming week, and block out a bit of time each day to get them done. Don't try and do them all in one day so that you can use the rest of the days for having fun; you will burn out and end up feeling more stressed than you started. You should have a balanced schedule for each day that includes some work time, some fun and socializing time, and some quiet unwinding time.

Here's an example of what a snippet of your schedule could look like:

# TEENS' GUIDE TO HEALTH AND MENTAL WELL...

8 a.m. - 4 p.m.: School (including traveling there and back)

4 p.m. - 5 p.m.: Have a snack and unwind

5 p.m. - 6:30 p.m.: Schoolwork

6:30 p.m. - 7 p.m.: Clean up bedroom, set the table for dinner, and do other chores

7 p.m. - 7:30 p.m.: Family dinner time

8 p.m. - 9 p.m.: Dance class.

9:15 p.m. - 11 p.m.: Cinema with friends

**Now, stick your completed planner on the wall, take a photo of it, and stick to it! Knowing what is coming up should help you to feel a little less stressed. If you've planned to work for an hour and haven't quite finished, you should put it to one side and finish it the next day. Having regular schoolwork sessions planned will mean that nothing should be done at the last minute and there'll be no need to rush anything. All Surprises Are Good**

Of course, there will be occasional times when your careful planning goes out the window. You might get an after-school detention, have an extra sports practice session scheduled at short notice, or fall out with friends who then uninvite you to a party. Dealing with unexpected changes can cause more stress; you'll find yourself with less time than you need, or more time and not knowing how to fill it!

Remind yourself that these changes aren't the end of the world. Why not keep a post-it note of extra activity ideas next to your planner to fill any time slots that unexpectedly open up? Things you don't usually get to do like reading a book in the bath, clearing out your wardrobe of old clothes, or catching up with friends or family members that you don't see regularly. And if your planned relaxation time ends up being work time or sports time, simply swap the blocks around. If your tennis lesson is moved from Monday to Thursday, whatever would have been in Thursday's slot now becomes your Monday activity.

## Making Choices

There are so many more opportunities for young people today that it can feel like you need to grab as many of them as you can or you'll be missing out. However, constantly being on the go doesn't leave you much time for relaxation and soon those hobbies and clubs you picked up will feel less enjoyable and more like a chore. Remember, you have ten different sports clubs to choose from because having that variety makes it more likely that you'll find one you like, not because you're expected to join them all. When I was at school, it was just football, athletics, or tennis—which I loved, but not everyone in my class was as sporty as me, and I remember a lot of kids struggling to get motivated chasing a ball around a muddy field in the middle of winter. Now, there are things like yoga, golf, trampolining, and volleyball that appeal to a much wider range of teenagers. Letting go of the idea that you have to do everything can be hugely freeing. Yes, if you want to have a different club every day, you can do it, but there's nothing to feel bad about if you don't.

The same is true for everything else in your life. If you accept every party invitation, you might find yourself without time to do anything else. And while having a part-time job can teach you about responsibility and how to manage your money, you don't want to spend all your spare time working or your schoolwork and social life will suffer. If you're lucky enough to have things to choose from, remember that it is a choice, and people will understand if you turn them down to spend time on your own mental health.

## How to Let It Go

Learning to relax and release any stress that has built up over the day will help you sleep better and feel more positive about yourself and your future. Your body is supposed to naturally lower your levels of cortisol and adrenaline, but sometimes it needs a little help—like squeezing a bottle to help it empty faster. Don't be tempted to go straight from homework to bed; you need a break between the two to draw a line under your day. Having a good bedtime routine can help you sleep better. I'm not just talking about brushing your teeth and turning out the light at a reasonable hour. There are relaxation activities you can incorporate that will give your de-stressing process a kick-start.

- Avoid screens for at least an hour before bedtime. Phone, tablet, and laptop screens emit blue light that can interfere with your body's natural time-keeping hormone melatonin. Melatonin levels rise when it gets dark and they prepare your body for sleep, but the wrong kind of artificial light prevents this from happening, meaning you spend longer tossing and turning before finally getting to sleep. When you're lying in the dark, your brain often fixates on stressful situations from the day and you may find yourself replaying them and feeling stressed out all over again. If you really must be using a screen late into the evening, turn on its blue light filter or buy one that clips over the top.

- End the day by writing your thoughts in a journal. You can buy blank ones or find journals and workbooks full of specifically designed exercises to help you process your thoughts from the day. If you don't feel comfortable talking about things with an adult, journaling is a great way to help you look at things differently. You might realize that things aren't as hopeless as they seem.

- If it's safe to do so, take a gentle evening walk around the neighborhood. Not a run, as this will raise your adrenaline levels. As you walk, don't be tempted to stare at your phone or listen to music; try and be in the moment. Notice the sights, sounds, and smells of your surroundings. This can be a really good way to ground yourself and get away from unhelpful thoughts.

- Read a book or listen to music or a podcast. You can do this in bed, on the sofa, or even in the bath! Make sure you're somewhere comfortable where you won't be disturbed for about half an hour. If you find it difficult to relax by being still, why not try a mindfulness coloring book, playing an instrument, drawing, crocheting, or anything else where you can focus on a small task? Doing something you enjoy at the end of the day will give you a nice hit of serotonin and leave you feeling happy and satisfied.

- Have a bedtime beauty routine. Treat yourself to some nice cleansers or face masks and take a few minutes every evening to physically wipe or wash away the day. This will have wonderful benefits for your skin as well as symbolically cleanse you of the day's worries.

The trick to all of these is to do them regularly and make them an essential part of your nightly routine. Soon, your body will recognize that a face mask or a walk is the signal to start winding down, and this will become the cue to start putting your body into sleep mode. Knowing that you have this powerful tool in your hands will mean that you can get to sleep even after the most horrible day.

# Chapter Five

## Dealing With Depression

*There is hope, even when your brain tells you there isn't.*
–John Green

Depression is probably the mental health disorder that has had the most publicity over the past twenty years, although many others are now catching up. Where stress and anxiety have some positive function—to keep you alert and safe, first from marauding predators, and now from missed deadlines and grumpy teachers—depression is not one of your body's natural functions gone wrong.

### More Than Just Feeling Sad

One common misconception with depression is that it's just a really intense form of feeling sad. You can feel a little bit sad about something for a short time, like dropping your ice cream on the floor, or deeply sad about something for a long time, like the death of a family member or friend. Even though feelings of deep sadness will linger for a long time, they will start to fade and eventually get better on their own. Feeling sad doesn't happen randomly, there's always a cause that makes you feel this way, and it's a normal reaction to have.

Depression, however, can start without an obvious cause, although there are some risk factors that can make you more likely to feel this way. Depression is a bit like a cataract on your soul: Everything seems dimmed and unexciting. You don't feel like doing anything, the whole world seems to slow down, and you feel completely hopeless. You might recognize those symptoms from chapter three when we talked about anxiety. Depression and anxiety often look and feel very similar, especially when you're a teenager, which can make it difficult for you to tell which disorder you are suffering from. However, a mental health professional will be able to diagnose you based on talking to you about your general mood, your life, and recent events.

**Depression or Anxiety?**

Depression is a mood disorder that affects the way you feel, whereas anxiety covers a group of behavioral disorders that can affect how you feel and what you do. These include phobias, OCD, panic attacks, and generalized anxiety disorder. It's quite common to have both anxiety and depression at the same time and they can both be treated with the same antidepressants and talk therapies.

One big difference between the two is that anxiety will make you feel worried or panicky about things, whereas depression will often make you feel nothing at all. If you feel on edge all the time, constantly restless, or afraid of what people are going to say or do, then it's more likely you are feeling more anxious than depressed.

## Causes and Symptoms

Another misconception that people have about depression is that it's caused by a hormonal imbalance—where there aren't enough of the chemicals in your brain that should make you feel happy and let you enjoy things. Yes, there can be a chemical element to depression, but there are other causes too, like having to deal with unexpected or unwanted changes in your life. You might develop mild depression after moving to a new school because you miss your friends and your old house, and you're finding it stressful to start again. In this scenario, there's nothing happening that will affect your brain chemistry and the best treatment for you will be to make new friends, join in with school activities, and decorate your bedroom so it feels like home.

Other illnesses can also trigger a bout of depression. If you suffer from a chronic illness like Crohn's Disease, diabetes, arthritis, lupus, or cancer, you will have days where you feel worse than others, often as a result of trying to do something fun or energetic. This can make you feel hopeless and worthless like your life is too difficult for you to enjoy yourself. Also, any illness that affects the brain, like epilepsy, could make you more likely to develop depressive symptoms.

Some medicines can also cause depression as a side effect. Doctors will look at your medical history to decide if you are at risk before they prescribe them to you, but sometimes there isn't another option. You can usually take antidepressants at the same time to try and minimize the effects. Illegal drugs and alcohol can also make you feel depressed, especially when taken frequently or in high doses. They interfere with the way your brain reacts to some hormones and chemicals that can lead to you feeling less happy more often. When doctors prescribe you a medication, they think very carefully about how it will make you feel, but if you take illegal drugs, you have no idea how they will affect you. Even taking something just once could cause you permanent damage and leave you with life-changing injuries, or even take your life from you altogether.

## Depression Risk Factors

I mentioned at the beginning of this chapter that there are some things that can make you more likely to develop depression at some stage in your life. These are called risk factors because they increase the risk. Experiencing one or more of these risk factors doesn't mean that you will definitely suffer from depression; in fact, many people go through lots of things on this list without experiencing a single depressive episode, while others will be depressed without dealing with any of them.

The key risk factors for depression are:

- being a victim of bullying

- having an existing mental health condition

- having a family history of mental health conditions

- having a physical disability, chronic pain, or serious illness

- abusing alcohol or illegal drugs

- feeling unstable at home due to moving house frequently, financial problems, parents splitting up, etc.

- witnessing or experiencing violence or abuse, either regularly or on a single occasion

- having problems at school; for example, failing classes or struggling to make friends

- coping with your sexual or gender identity without support or in an environment where you would be persecuted if you came out

- feeling lonely or isolated

## What Depression Feels Like

At the core of any episode of depression is a persistent low mood where you don't just feel sad, you target yourself with negative thoughts and feelings. You feel worthless, helpless, and guilty that other people might be worrying about you when you don't deserve it, and you may also feel that everyone else would be better off if you weren't around. These aren't the only symptoms, but they are the main ones, and they really help you to understand the difference between depression and sadness. Here are two further examples. See if you can identify which person is suffering from depression.

Avery is supposed to be getting ready for her best friend Lin's party, but she is lying on her bed scrolling through social media and looking at her ex's account. She feels exhausted and every time she thinks about getting dressed she starts to feel anxious. Then she feels guilty because she knows Lin really wants her there, but she just can't face it. Avery messages Lin and tells her that she isn't feeling well and she can't make it. Lin texts her straight back with a puppy GIF and tells her she hopes she feels better soon. That makes Avery feel even worse.

Amelia's cat has passed away. She keeps bursting into tears when she remembers him or when she sees his spot on the chair is empty. She doesn't want to go out with her friends this weekend and cancels plans. Instead, she and her sister watch a movie in their pjs and binge-eat popcorn and ice cream. At school on Monday, she is quieter than usual and has her lunch in the classroom instead of sitting with her friends in the canteen.

Amelia is feeling sad about something that happened, but Avery is feeling depressed and down about herself. Did you spot some of the other symptoms of depression in there too? Like other mental health disorders, depression can have both physical and mental symptoms.

Physical symptoms include:

- feeling exhausted and tired, regardless of how much sleep you get or how much activity you do

- sleeping too much or not enough

- losing weight or gaining weight without trying to
- finding it difficult to concentrate or focus on anything, even stuff you usually enjoy
- feeling like you're moving and thinking in slow motion
- headaches, backaches, and other physical problems that don't have an obvious explanation

Mental symptoms include:

- feeling irritable, annoyed, or angry for no reason
- nothing feeling fun or enjoyable anymore
- lacking in motivation to do anything, even if you know it would be good for you or it was something you used to enjoy
- criticism from other people making you feel really upset, even if it's something light or even said as a joke
- continuing to think about mistakes you made and times when things went wrong
- suicidal thoughts and thinking about death

If you find you are having thoughts about hurting yourself, it's really important that you talk to an adult you can trust. However worthless and helpless you feel right now, there are solutions and treatments out there for you that can help, but it's the depression that makes it hard for you to see that, or to imagine a future where you feel okay again. No one is going to be angry with you for feeling this way.

## Once You Ask For Help

Getting help for your depression is pretty easy. There are lots of treatment options available. Some work by stopping you from feeling negative and others help you to change the way you think about things. Your doctor might want you to try a combination of medication and talk therapy, or they might decide that you only need one or the other. It depends on what kind of depression you have, and a trained medical professional will be able to diagnose this for you, although it might take them a few conversations.

## Antidepressants

There are different types of antidepressants and, although they all relieve the symptoms of depression, they target different chemicals in your brain. Having higher serotonin levels usually makes you feel more positive and happy, so many antidepressants aim to stop your brain from reabsorbing serotonin and getting rid of it.

The antidepressants that have the fewest side effects are called SSRIs. These are usually the first type your doctor will prescribe you and they include fluoxetine (Prozac), sertraline (Zoloft), and paroxetine (Paxil).

Another set of antidepressants are called SNRIs and these increase the levels of both serotonin and norepinephrine in your brain. You might be prescribed one of these if SSRIs don't work for you or if you are taking other prescription medication, as they don't really interact with other drugs. Some SNRIs include venlafaxine (Effexor) and duloxetine (Cymbalta). (Bennington-Castro, 2018).

There are three more types, but they are much less common. All antidepressants can have some unpleasant side effects—like nausea, sleeplessness, and a dry mouth—but these might only last for a few weeks, or they can be something that you try and get used to. For really bad side effects, your doctor could offer you more pills, or something to stop you from feeling sick.

Unfortunately, there is still a stigma surrounding antidepressants that can prevent some people from taking them. Some people believe that antidepressants make you unable to feel anything and you'll end up acting like a zombie. In reality, the number of people who end up feeling emotionally numbed after taking antidepressants is much smaller than the number of people who are helped by them. Proper communication with your doctor is really important, and if you find yourself struggling with side effects you should tell them so that they can prescribe you a different medication.

## Talk Therapy

Antidepressants can help you start to feel better, but they work best when you also use therapy to treat the cause of your depression. Talk therapies are where you and a licensed counselor or therapist discuss some of the problems you are having and they suggest ways that you can help yourself. This often involves teaching you how to think more positively in situations that make you anxious or depressed. For example, if a friend cancels plans with you because they say they feel ill, you might start to feel negative about yourself. You might think: They really canceled because they don't like you, they have plans with other friends instead, and they're all laughing about you behind your back. Your therapist can help you control these thoughts so that they don't send you into a depression spiral, meaning the next time plans change, you won't instantly assume the worst.

Changing the way you think about things can stop you from entering a depressive episode. Imagine you're in a restaurant and the waiter keeps filling up your glass of water. Every time you empty it, or nearly empty it, they reappear and top it up again. They don't even ask you if you want more, they just do it. That's how it can feel when you're battling depression: Everything you do to help empty your glass (like exercising, eating right, and sleeping properly) doesn't matter once the next set of negative thoughts come along to fill it up again. Antidepressants can help you empty the glass faster, and talk therapies can stop the waiter from turning up again.

## Supporting Yourself and Your Friends

I've already mentioned that one of the key symptoms of depression is feeling hopeless or worthless, and this often interferes with your ability to do anything. After all, why would you bother going to the movies if you're not going to enjoy the film (hopeless), or have a shower when it won't make you look or feel better (worthless)? Putting any effort into your own comfort or enjoyment seems pointless, but actually, you will start to feel a bit better for it. Because depression also tends to bring emotional and physical fatigue, the amount of energy needed to actually start a positive activity might seem gargantuan, but it's like pushing your bike up a hill—once you get to the top, the rest is easy.

### Emotional First Aid

Make yourself a list of five activities that you enjoy but don't take a lot of energy (on a normal day). This is going

## TEENS' GUIDE TO HEALTH AND MENTAL WELL...

to be your first aid checklist. When you find yourself in a depression funk and unable to muster the motivation to do something, reach for your list and work through the activities. The lift you will get from this might then give you the energy to achieve something more taxing, like homework, walking the dog, or having a conversation with a friend.

Some suggestions for your list:

- Spend at least 10 minutes with an adult coloring book. It sounds silly, but it helps you to relax by calming the thoughts flying around your brain and focusing your energy on something creative instead. You can get all sorts of coloring books, from repeating patterns to comedy cartoons, so there should be something to suit your tastes.

- Paint your nails. Like the coloring book, it focuses your brain on a single task, allowing stray, unhelpful thoughts to float away.

- Read a chapter of a book or listen to a chapter of an audiobook. Audiobooks are great because you can listen to them while lying down in the dark if you find life at the moment overstimulating.

- Sit or walk through nature for 10 minutes. Connecting with nature can help to slow your heart rate, regulate your breathing, and lower your blood pressure. Even sitting on a balcony or backyard will help. If you haven't got a quiet outside space, you can listen to nature sounds, like rain, waves, or jungle insects. It isn't quite the same, but it will still give you some relaxing benefits.

- Take a shower and use your favorite body wash, shampoo, and any other fancy scrubs you want. The added sensation of hot water will distract you from your thoughts and help to ground you in the moment.

- Listen to happy and uplifting music. Make yourself a "cheer up" playlist of uptempo songs with happy memories or associations. Listening to sad music, while you might think it's appropriate, won't do anything to change your mood; it will only reinforce it.

- Dance to your playlist! If the songs are catchy enough, you probably won't be able to stop yourself.

- Watch an episode of your favorite sitcom. Keep it light and fluffy and there's nothing wrong with watching the same episode over and over again—our brains like familiarity and it's reassuring to know what's coming next because it prevents anxiety.

- Text or call a friend who you know will respond. Talking with someone, even if it's about nothing in particular, can lift your mood and make you feel more positive about yourself.

## Reaching Out

What's the point of the internet letting us be in constant communication with each other if we don't use it for good? Teens are pretty good at supporting each other, but your friends can only help you if you talk to them about how you're feeling or let them know what you need. You don't need to explain any more than you are comfortable with, but I bet your friends will be only too eager to help you out. No one likes to think of their friends feeling down, and I bet you'd feel pretty bad if you found out your friend was feeling depressed and you hadn't done anything to help them.

Pick a couple of friends that you trust and tell them how they can support you in person, not over text. You could try saying something like:

- If I call you but I'm not very chatty, please just talk to me about something you enjoy. I'll join in if I can, but it might be enough for me to just listen.

- If you get a text from me that says "Cheer up needed," please spam me with stupid videos and memes, or call me and just talk about anything random.

- Please don't stop inviting me to things, even if I miss a few. I still like to feel included and know what's going on.

- Just because I can't handle going out, doesn't always mean I want to be alone. If I cancel or decline plans, please suggest just coming over to watch a movie.

## Being There For Others

Support networks work both ways. If you notice that a friend has been quiet or withdrawn recently, you could reach out to them and ask them what they need from you. Maybe some of the above suggestions are things you could do for them, or maybe they want someone to talk to about their problems. It can be difficult to take the first step to ask for help, but if you offer it first, you can make that step much easier for someone else. It can be as simple as sending a DM on their socials, something like, "Hi, I haven't seen you posting much recently. I wanted to see if you were okay. Do you want to talk about anything?"

Remember, if a friend confides in you and you're worried about their health or their safety, you shouldn't keep it to yourself. It's okay to tell a trusted adult, like your caregivers or a teacher at school, that you have a friend who is struggling. They should be able to help you support your friend in getting the help and advice that they need. Your friend might be angry that you didn't keep their confidence, but when they are feeling better, they will realize that you only wanted to help them. At the end of the day, would you rather your friend was angry with you but alive and well, or they had hurt themselves and nobody helped them?

**Spread the word!**
*Thank you for coming this far. If you're enjoying this book, please consider sharing your thoughts by leaving an honest review. Your review, which will be greatly appreciated by me, may help others on their respective journeys to adulthood*
*Thank you,*
*Kev"*

**Teens' Guide to Health and Mental Wellness**

 US Review

Click here

Thank you for your review 👍

**Teens' Guide to Health and Mental Wellness**

 UK Review

Click here

Thank you for your review 👍

# Chapter Six

## Bad Coping Strategies

*Promise me you'll always remember — you're braver than you believe, and stronger than you seem, and smarter than you think.* –Christopher Robin (Winnie the Pooh)

We've looked at three specific conditions that can contribute to bad mental health, but they aren't the only causes. Sometimes your mental health can be affected by short-term problems that cause a spike in cortisol or a dip in dopamine. When your mental health suddenly changes—whether for the better or worse—it can make you feel like you are being swept along for the ride. That can be a rather scary feeling, even for adults. Imagine if your arm suddenly stuck up in the air without you asking it to. Wouldn't you feel alarmed, embarrassed, and start to wonder what else your body might do by itself? Your mental health changing by itself can feel just as strange.

You can control your mental health—if you couldn't, there'd be no point in me writing this book!—however, it isn't a simple or quick process. If you feel hungry, you eat a snack, and you feel better, but there's no equally fast way to completely stop yourself from feeling depressed or anxious. However, that doesn't stop people from trying, and quite often this leads to dangerous or harmful behavior that seems to give a quick result but is only either a temporary fix or actually ends up doing more damage in the long run.

## A Question of Control

A very common symptom of low mental health is feeling that you aren't in control of your life. Your body isn't doing what you want it to do, you aren't feeling the way you want to feel, and sometimes you don't even react the way you mean to. Small things upset you in big ways, your favorite hobbies aren't fun anymore, and even though you hate being this way, there doesn't seem to be anything you can do about it. It's a very isolating feeling, especially if you're not used to talking about mental health, but it's actually very common, especially for teenagers. There are so many changes going on inside your brain that it's completely reasonable to expect it to malfunction.

# TEENS' GUIDE TO HEALTH AND MENTAL WELL...

There's a reason why your phone, laptop, and gaming console don't let you use them while they're installing updates—if only your brain gave you the same option!

When it feels like your life is getting out of control, it's only natural to want to get that control back. Even though you're starting to be more independent, the adults in your life still have quite a lot of control over where you go, what you do, and when it all happens. If you lash out against some of their rules in order to try and regain control of something, there are often consequences or punishments. It might momentarily feel good to stay out too late, or ditch school to go shopping, but you will be feeling even worse when you get caught and end up grounded.

One thing that teenagers and young adults often resort to when feeling out of control, is trying to find ways to control their own body. After all, it's their body that is making them feel adrift, so it makes sense, right? Also, it's not something that their parents can often see, or are likely to punish them for. Some things are harmless—like getting a new haircut or dying it a fun color—but others—like over-exercising and restricting food—can lead to long-term health issues.

## Behaviors to Avoid

Having mental health highs and lows is a normal part of life, but it can take some getting used to. Have you ever had a wonderful day—maybe a fun vacation, a birthday party, or got some excellent exam results—and then felt lethargic and floppy the next day? This is a natural low that follows a period of heightened excitement and enjoyment. It's nothing to worry about, and you'll probably be over it by the following day.

However, for some people, these highs and lows are less predictable, and the lows don't pass as quickly as they would like. Even when they do things that they usually enjoy, if they're in a low mood and their mental health is in a bad state, then their brain won't be getting the usual hit of happy hormones. This, then, means that their chosen activity doesn't make them feel as good as they were hoping, which can lead to trying to find more extreme activities that will reduce the low feelings.

In chapter two, I already covered some ways that you can naturally improve your mental health, and I'm going to cover a lot more in chapters seven and eight, but for now, we're going to look at some behaviors that will not, under any circumstances, help your mental wellness. The following is a list of common responses to bad mental health that teenagers seem particularly drawn to. You will come across characters struggling with these issues in popular TV shows, movies, and books, and even see personalities on social media talking about their own experiences. Some adults like to claim that these images give teenagers bad ideas, but these behaviors existed long before the media. I am including this disclaimer before continuing because I want to drill home how damaging some of these behaviors can be, and how quickly they can go from an occasional release to a debilitating habit.

## Social Isolation

Quite often the sources of anxiety and stress are external factors, like worrying about schoolwork, friendship struggles, or feeling uncomfortable around strangers. Avoiding these issues can quickly remove the triggers of your low mood, but it won't do anything to change how you'll feel when you have to face that situation again. In fact, it can make things worse, because hiding away in your room and reducing your social contact is going to cause a drop in your serotonin levels, increasing your depressive feelings. Humans are social beings and we need connections with others to feel happy. Some of us find it easier to socialize than others, but being socially awkward doesn't mean that you don't need that contact.

## Controlling and Restricting Food

We all know that we need to eat in order to live, and most people have a good idea of which foods are healthier than others. When you look at it logically, it seems strange to think that some people will refuse to eat as a way to make themselves feel better. But as I mentioned above, sometimes you can feel so out of control of your emotions that you will try to gain control over something else to compensate. It's easy for most teenagers to skip meals, especially if they're rushing to school in the morning and then choose not to make or have lunch.

Some people find they naturally lose their appetite when they get anxious, so not eating becomes a natural response. Others will feel hungry, but knowing this is a feeling they have caused—unlike the emotional ups and downs they have no control over—can help them feel calmer and more in control. However, in reality, they haven't gained any control over what initially caused their mental health to drop, and restricting food, particularly during puberty when your body does so much growing and developing, can lead to physical problems. Remember, it's not just food your body is losing, but all the vitamins and minerals needed for good bone growth, healthy teeth, a strong immune system, and properly functioning organs. Food-controlling habits can also lead to the development of an eating disorder. Ninety-five percent of eating disorders begin before the age of 25 (McCarthy, 2022), and they can take years to overcome.

**Over-Exercising**

Often linked with food restriction, over-exercising is another way to feel more in control of your body. Of course, when done properly, physical exercise is good for you. It improves your mental health by increasing dopamine production, keeping you fit, improving muscle tone, and burning fat stores. Most people start exercising regularly as a way to lose weight—a good way to feel better about themselves and lift low self-esteem—but that initial good feeling of making a positive change can wear off. Soon, it takes more and more exercise to feel the same high, while also becoming harder and harder to lose weight once you reach a healthy value. This is where over-exercising starts to become damaging to your health.

Over-exercising can lead to a greater number of physical injuries, and unless you stop exercising, you won't get the chance to heal properly. Also, losing too much weight will mean your body has no energy stores to use up, so it will start to either shut down non-vital systems or break down muscles for energy instead. If you menstruate, over-exercising can cause irregular periods, or make them stop altogether, which could affect your fertility—you might not be thinking about that now, but when you're older, it isn't something to easily fix.

## Reinventing Yourself

You might have heard the old expression "a change is as good as a rest," which alludes to how refreshing it can be to do something different. Lots of people find that they like to change something to make them feel better, either after a breakup, when starting a new school, or as a way to lift their mental health. Like everything else on this list, making a change in your appearance, or the decor of your room, can initially make you feel more cheerful, but it does nothing to address the underlying issues affecting your mental health. While there's nothing wrong with a new haircut or wardrobe, some changes, like getting piercings and tattoos, are much more permanent, not to mention painful. Drastic changes are also going to draw a lot of attention to you, which might make you feel more anxious, especially if people make negative comments.

## Vaping

Most people are aware of the negative effects that smoking cigarettes can have on your health, including increasing your risk of developing heart disease, lung disease, and cancer. There's a big misconception around vaping and eCigarettes that they are a safer alternative to cigarettes, and this has led to them appealing to teenagers. Many brands of vape and eLiquid still contain high levels of nicotine, which is addictive and can affect the way that your brain develops if you use it as a teenager (CDC, 2022).

Some people vape when they feel stressed because the nicotine makes your body immediately feel more relaxed. However, this feeling is temporary, and once it wears off you will feel stressed again. It's not a proper cure, just like eating ice cream doesn't really heal heartbreak, but it can leave you with some nasty after effects. There are chemicals in eCigarette smoke that can cause heavy metal poisoning and others that can leave you with incurable lung diseases. According to the CDC (2022), around 14% of high school students and more than 3% of middle school students vape regularly. That's a lot of chemical exposure at a young age, for something that doesn't have any lasting benefits. Vaping is so new that scientists have no idea what the long-term effects could be and they're still doing research to find out exactly how much damage it does to your lungs.

## Substance Abuse

Drinking alcohol or taking illegal drugs can change the way you feel and mask the symptoms of low mental health, but the effects are always temporary. The more you drink, the quicker you will build up a tolerance, meaning you will need two beers to feel the same way you used to after one. This is how alcohol problems get out of control, and you go from needing one drink to feel better, to needing a whole case. Also, alcohol is actually a depressant. This means that it slows you down and helps you relax, but in larger quantities, it will make you feel more depressed because it affects the way your brain receives messages and processes its chemicals. Additionally, one of the things that alcohol slows down is your ability to recognize danger and assess situations. This makes it much more likely that you will do something stupid while under the influence, and that could lead to a serious injury.

Some drugs are also depressants while others are stimulants; you might hear these referred to as uppers and downers. Prescription medications that are designed to treat depression and anxiety work by improving the amount of neurotransmitters in your brain. Illegal drugs affect your dopamine receptors, making you feel happy or relaxed and craving more of the same feeling. But unlike genuine happiness or relaxation, this fades quickly, often leaving you with a lower mood than before you started. Also, unlike prescription medications, illegal drugs are often mixed with other chemicals that can be poisonous or harmful. There are also no set recipes, meaning one pill might be much stronger than another, even though the main ingredient is the same.

Have you ever tried Tabasco or hot sauce? Now, imagine someone hands you a bunch of identical bottles and tells you that some are stronger than others, but you don't know which ones, or how strong they are. Would you still eat it, even if there was a chance it could be so strong that it physically burned your mouth? It only takes one bad drug to cause irreparable damage, a risk definitely not worth taking considering there is no chance of it helping your mental health in the long run.

## Cutting and Self-Harm

Self-harm covers any methods that are used to intentionally cause yourself pain. Most commonly people think of cutting—using a razor or other blade to cut or scratch your arm, thigh, or other body parts—but it can also include burning yourself, scratching, pinching, or picking at your skin, pulling out hair, hitting your head with your hands or against objects, piercing your skin, and pushing objects underneath your skin. None of that sounds like a lot of fun, so why is it that some people feel the need to resort to this behavior?

It's essentially a distraction technique. You might be feeling really strong emotions that you can't get under control and are unbearable, like deep sadness or burning anger, and so you think that the only way to not feel that anymore is to interrupt or override it with physical pain. When my friend's son was a frustrated toddler, he used to bang his head against the wall when he was upset about something and didn't have the words to explain how he was feeling. It seems to be an instinctive reaction that humans have, to replace an uncontrollable pain with one that they understand better.

There are websites on the internet that seem to encourage self-harming by showing teenagers ways to supposedly do it safely. But there is never a safe way to hurt yourself. Self-harm can leave you with permanent scars, which may bring questions from others if they are in a visible place. If you cut too deeply, you risk suffering from blood loss and needing medical attention. Any time you break the skin, you risk exposing yourself to bacteria and contracting an infection, even if you think you have used clean equipment or sterile wipes.

**Extreme Risk Taking**

Every day we make lots of small decisions that are designed to keep us safe: blowing on your coffee before taking a sip, looking both ways before crossing the road, tying a loose shoelace before you trip... the list goes on. Sometimes we also have to make decisions about risks and balance whether the reward will be worth it. Do you sneak out to the party you've been told you can't go to? Do you ask someone out, even though they might say no? Do you apply to the college you want, even though it's far away?

Generally, these risks are still safe—even if you get in trouble with your caregivers for something, it's unlikely you'll come to real harm. When your mental health is very low, it's hard to feel positive emotions from normal activities like watching a comedy or spending time with your friends. Instead, some people turn to risky activities to feel better, and they will keep looking for bigger and bigger ones in order to keep feeling excited. Sneaking out to one party soon becomes staying out all night, every night, and spending time with other risk-takers.

This becomes a problem because, as you seek bigger risks, you make more unwise decisions, and these significantly increase your chances of being injured, assaulted, or exposed to substances or activities that you would normally avoid. Putting yourself in danger in order to feel brighter is never a good trade-off.

## Sexual Promiscuity

As a subsection of risk-taking, this one warrants its own mention. Cultural, social, and personal attitudes toward sex vary greatly depending on where you live and how you were raised, but unhealthy and harmful sexual practices are universal: sleeping with people you don't know, under the influence of alcohol or drugs, in unsafe environments, without explicit consent, and without using adequate protection. Never mind the worry of becoming pregnant or impregnating your partner (if you are of different genders), regardless of who you sleep with, you risk contracting an STD—and there are still some, like herpes and HIV that have no cure. One mistake could be with you for life.

## A Vicious Circle

While all of the behaviors talked about in this chapter can offer a short-term high, hopefully, you can recognize that they don't do anything concrete to change the situation you are in. A new hair color can make you feel great for a few days, but it can't take away the causes of your stress or depression. You might feel less anxious about making friends after a couple of drinks, but it won't make you feel less anxious the next time you meet those people sober.

All of the coping mechanisms listed above are called maladaptive strategies. They seek to relieve the symptoms of low mental health without changing anything else. In the next chapter, I'm going to introduce you to some adaptive strategies. These are designed to help you resolve the problems that are damaging your mental health, giving you a more permanent lift to your mood. They aren't quick fixes, but they are the only long-lasting ones.

# TEENS' GUIDE TO HEALTH AND MENTAL WELL...

# Chapter Seven

## Building Your Wellness Toolbox

*Sometimes self care is exercise and eating right. Sometimes it's spending time with loved ones or taking a nap. And sometimes it's watching an entire season of TV in one weekend while you lounge around in your pajamas. Whatever soothes your soul.* –Nanea Hoffman

Mental health problems among teenagers are growing. It doesn't matter which statistics you look at or what reports you read; they all say the same things. We're getting better at talking about our mental health, but there are still people who are afraid to speak out and get the help that they need. This means that far too many teenagers are still struggling silently and alone.

# TEENS' GUIDE TO HEALTH AND MENTAL WELL...

However, there has still been a significant increase in the number of young people seeking help from professional services, and that means that some people are having to wait a long time for a referral, treatment, or admission to the hospital. What do you do while you're waiting? In this chapter, I'm going to introduce you to some more activities and exercises you can do at home to help manage your mood. Some are linked to approved therapies like CBT and DBT; others take a more alternative route to wellness, and it's for you to experiment and decide what helps you the most. At the end of the day, if something works to lift you up, regardless of how silly it sounds or whether it's been prescribed by a professional, it's the right treatment for you.

Here's an example from a friend's teenage daughter:

When I get stressed or frustrated, I find it difficult to control how I'm feeling and I end up doing irrational things. All I want to do is throw things around or run out of the house—and I usually can't do either. I have a three-song playlist that I put on as loud as I can that I know helps me to work out my frustrations and calm down. I air-drum along to the first song; it's fast and angry, and it matches my mood. I can thrash about and pretend I'm smashing things. The second song is still fast but it's more upbeat, so I start dancing instead. I think that moving around really helps me to calm down. My third song is slower and has powerful lyrics that remind me that I'm in control.

By the time I've listened to my playlist, I've worked out a lot of my anger and I can think about what happened, or what to do next, in a much calmer way.

## Talking Helps

I cannot emphasize this enough: If you don't talk about your problems, they won't get better. Mental health disorders like depression and anxiety are not like the flu; you can't just stay in bed eating chicken soup for a week and then be over it. One thing these disorders do is make you feel there is something wrong with you because you are struggling, and one of the best ways to overcome that is to find out that you are not alone. Having low mental health can make you feel isolated, so to be able to speak to other people in the same situation is really powerful. Your doctor might be able to put you in touch with a local peer support group where you can meet other teenagers and young people who have been where you are. You don't have to speak up until you're ready, but it can be helpful just listening to other people talk about their daily struggles and what they do to help themselves.

You might find that your school has a peer support system already in place. It's becoming increasingly common for schools to offer mental health spaces and places for students to talk about their worries. If not, perhaps you could suggest setting one up. Schools often recruit older students as learning mentors or friendship advocates, so why shouldn't there be mental health champions too?

Talking to others also helps you to get another point of view on a situation. Let's say you're feeling anxious about having to give an oral report in class and all you can focus on is the different ways that it could go wrong. Talking about your fears with others can help you realize that some of the things you were worried about are really unlikely to happen, some of them won't be as bad as you think, and some could actually be a good thing. Other people can also help you to refocus your thoughts on the positives and how you'll feel a sense of achievement afterward.

Finally, talking to others is absolutely necessary if you want to start accessing help for your mental health problems. Maybe you want a friend to go with you to see the school counselor or to provide moral support when you talk to your parents. Or maybe you don't know who to go to or how to get help, but a trusted adult will be able to help you find that information out.

## Behavioral Therapies

Talking to friends and trusted adults is a great first step, but if you need more help improving your mental health, you might want to look into some therapy sessions with a licensed counselor. Talk therapies give you a chance to tell your therapist exactly how you are feeling, what upsets you or makes you anxious, and how long you've been feeling this way. They might ask you about things that happened in the past or guide you to think more deeply about why you think a particular situation or action affects you. Sessions can be quite draining and emotional, but they can also feel like a huge release and leave you feeling uplifted and unburdened. It all depends on your therapist and the approach they take.

There are a few different talk therapies that are commonly used to treat mental health disorders. The main two are called cognitive behavioral therapy and dialectical behavioral therapy. They both help you overcome mental health issues by examining your behavior and getting you to focus on positive and helpful behaviors rather than negative thoughts and actions.

## Cognitive Behavioral Therapy

CBT is usually the first behavioral therapy that is suggested, as it's effective at treating a large number of mental health disorders, including eating disorders, anxiety disorders, depression, and ADHD. A course of CBT will encourage you to analyze negative patterns of behavior and thinking that appear in certain situations. One example of this is feeling anxious about talking to new people because you assume that they won't like you. CBT can help you to change the way you think and make it easier for you to talk to new people. Your therapist will get you to examine why you assume they won't like you, what has happened in the past to make you feel this way, and then ask you to think about times when the opposite was true.

CBT often involves you continuing the work outside of the therapist's office. In the example above, your therapist might ask you to talk to a number of new people as your homework, and then next session you would talk about how you felt each time. CBT is highly effective and there's lots of medical evidence to show that it works to help you make real, long-term changes to how you think and behave, as long as you put the work in.

## Decatastrophizing

When you feel depressed or anxious, you'll probably find yourself struggling with unhelpful thoughts that make the situation much worse. Left unchecked, your brain will come up with a slew of extreme and terrible scenarios that it convinces you will come true if you answer that phone call, miss your homework deadline, or go to the party. This is known as catastrophizing—making everything into a catastrophe.

Catastrophizing makes you feel like doing nothing (usually) is the best option. If you stay in your room, nothing bad can happen to you. However, this also means that nothing good can happen either. A piano won't fall on your head, but you also won't find a winning lottery ticket. In reality, avoiding everything bad that could happen to you just isn't practical. You'll end up missing out on a lot of fun things too.

CBT can help you examine your fearful thoughts and show you that what you're worried about is unlikely to happen, and if it does, the consequences won't be as bad as you think. This process is called decatastrophizing, and it works by getting you to ask yourself a series of analytical questions and really think about your answers. Here are the decatastrophizing questions, along with an example to show you how it works. You can jot your answers down in a journal or notebook to start with, and eventually, you will be able to do this process in your head.

1. What situation is worrying you?

2. What could happen that you are worried about? Identify your fear.

3. How likely is it that this will happen? Think about past experiences and give as much information as you can to back up your decision.

4. What is the worst that can happen as a result of your fear coming true?

5. What's most likely to happen if your fear comes true?

6. If your fear does come true, how do you think you will feel after a) one week, b) one month, and c) one year?

Here's an example from Daniel, a 14-year-old student who wants to try out for the school swim team.

1. What situation is worrying you?

    a. I put my name down for the swim team trials and I've been invited to the pool next week, but now just thinking about going makes me feel sick.

2. What could happen that you are worried about? Identify your fear.

    a. I'm worried that something will go wrong and I'll embarrass myself. What if I'm so much worse than everyone else there and they all laugh at me? What if I get so nervous I throw up in the pool?

3. How likely is it that this will happen? Think about past experiences and give as much information as you can to back up your decision.

    a. I know that tryouts are really popular and

there aren't a lot of spaces on the team, so there must be lots of people each year who don't make it. That probably means that the coaches are really nice about it and wouldn't let anyone tease the kids, even if they were awful. I've been nervous at competitions before and I always feel better once I'm in the water, even when I've been feeling really sick, so I probably won't throw up in the pool after all.

4. What is the worst that can happen as a result of your fear coming true?

    a. If everyone laughs at me I'll feel so embarrassed that I'll probably never swim again. I'll also be too anxious to go to school and will have to transfer somewhere else where people don't know me.

5. What's most likely to happen if your fear comes true?

    a. The coaches will stop people from laughing and give them a detention. I'll feel awkward for a few days but no one outside of the swim team will really know what happened and soon everyone will be talking about something else anyway.

6. If your fear does come true, how do you think you will feel after a) one week, b) one month, and c) one year?

   a. After a week, I might still feel embarrassed. After a month, people will probably have stopped talking about it. After a year, it won't matter anymore. I might not feel like swimming for a bit, but I really enjoy it so I don't think anything that happens will make me give it up completely.

## Dialectical Behavioral Therapy

DBT is a newer form of behavioral therapy and it is often used to treat more extreme mental health disorders like borderline personality disorder or where someone is having persistent suicidal thoughts. Rather than try and change the way you behave, DBT concentrates on teaching you new skills and arming you with new strategies to help you cope with your emotions. It is based on the idea of accepting that there are some things you cannot change and that you can learn to cope with these situations without feeling triggered.

There are four central concepts to DBT and they all work alongside each other. You can learn some of them from your therapist, others by teaching yourself using workbooks, and some from attending skills groups and workshops. These key concepts are:

- mindfulness: focusing on what is happening right now—actions, sounds conversations—and accepting everything without judgment, overreacting, or getting overwhelmed

- regulating your emotions: trying to have the right level of emotional response to something and learning how to calm yourself down quickly if you didn't

- effectively interacting with others: making sure you can communicate your needs to others so they can help you meet them

- tolerating distress: how to deal with the emotional and physical symptoms of being uncomfortable or anxious so that your discomfort doesn't make you feel worse

DBT can be really effective when you are dealing with lots of trauma, rather than a persistent low mood. An example would be if there was arguing or violence at home or a breakdown in your caregivers' relationship. These situations are likely to cause multiple occasions where you feel stressed or anxious and probably have you thinking and worrying about the future. DBT skills can help you to manage your feelings—for example, not panicking every time you hear shouting—so that you don't feel overwhelmed.

## Urge Surfing

CBT concentrates on changing your thinking so you don't find yourself getting anxious anymore, whereas DBT teaches you how to cope with triggering situations when they do occur. This can be really useful in the short term, perhaps alongside CBT therapy, because you're still going to find yourself in uncomfortable situations while you're working on your unhelpful thoughts.

One technique that DBT has to help you is called urge surfing. No, it isn't a new beach sport; it refers to what you should be doing when you get the sudden desire to do something. We all get urges, from wanting to eat a chocolate bar to needing to clean the bathroom, but some of them can be hurtful and destructive, such as the urge to drink or the urge to shout. Negative urges often pop up in a stressful situation and they can be really strong, but urge surfing helps you to understand that they are temporary and will pass without being met, unlike a real need like being hungry, thirsty, or needing the toilet—if you ignore one of these, it will only get stronger.

There are four main steps to urge surfing:

1. Acknowledge your urge. At this stage, it is probably still growing and once you accept that it's an urge and you're going to feel it, you can then start to deal with those feelings.

2. Accept how you're feeling, even if it's unpleasant. Your urge will get stronger if you don't respond to it and this can be frustrating and uncomfortable, but these feelings won't hurt you.

3. Remind yourself that the urge will pass. It is not something that you have to give in to, even if it seems like the urge will never go away. You can try and distract yourself by finding other things to do, talking to people, or getting away from your triggers.

4. Eventually, the urge will pass. Acknowledge that you managed your feelings, you didn't give in to the urge, and nothing bad happened. In fact, by not giving in to the urge, you might even find that something good has happened.

Here's an example of urge surfing from Shawna, a 17-year-old student who has been struggling with the urge to cut herself when she feels anxious.

*It's been a really stressful day today. Ma had to work late, which meant I had to pick my brother up from his after-school club, cook dinner, and help him with his home-*

*work before I even got started on my own. He wouldn't go to bed and I shouted at him, which made him cry. Now I feel really guilty and I'm trying to concentrate on studying for my geography exam when the urge to cut hit me. Last year I would have given in, but my therapist helped me to see how it isn't really helpful and so I'm trying to stop.*

*The urge starts by making my wrists itch, like all the guilt and stress I'm feeling needs me to let it out. The more I ignore it, the more twitch and uncomfortable my skin feels. I keep telling myself that I can handle the discomfort, that it's only an urge and not actually my wrists about to explode. I have some sweatbands that I put over my wrists—the feeling of the material helps to muffle the feeling from the urge.*

*Ma isn't home yet, so I can't go for a run—something I find really helpful in beating an urge because it takes me away from scissors or knives in the house, and it also makes me feel good to sprint as fast as I can down the road and back again. Instead, I put on my headphones and stick on my favorite album by The Weeknd. Focusing on the music is a great distraction—I even get up and dance a little. By the time the album is finished, the urge has completely gone. I didn't even notice it seeping away; it was just gone. I managed to get a bit more studying done and then decided I needed an early night.*

## Alternative Therapies and Medicines

Mental health treatments come in all shapes and sizes. This is because we all find different things funny, uplifting, and enjoyable, just as we all have different triggers for stress, anxiety, and depression. Treatments like antidepressant medication and counseling work for the vast majority of people, but there are other alternative therapies and medicines that can work alongside these conventional treatments that can help you relax, unwind, and calm down. Some of these might even be recommended by your family doctor or counselor.

## Aromatherapy

Aromatherapy uses essential oils—which are all natural and extracted from plants—to affect your mood. The oils are supposed to be absorbed or breathed in, so you can put a couple of drops in the bath or in a diffuser, or you can rub them into your skin. Some aromatherapy oils, like lavender, bergamot, and sandalwood, can help you feel more relaxed and less anxious.

Unless you know there's a plant that you're allergic to—in which case, don't buy that particular oil—there's a pretty low risk of any side effects or reactions to essential oils. They aren't safe to be eaten though, so make sure you keep them away from food and drinks, and definitely don't be tempted to add a few drops to your drinking water.

Essential oils can be bought from the pharmacy, a herbal food store, or online.

## Yoga

I've already included a few easy yoga routines in chapter two to get you started with this ancient Indian practice. Yoga combines breathing exercises with stretches and balances to help your physical and mental health at the same time. It's really easy to adapt to your level of ability by choosing gentle or challenging stretches and changing the length of your workouts. Sometimes you might just feel like doing some breathing exercises and restorative poses to help you relax and unwind, but other days you might want more of a workout.

Yoga classes are becoming more popular and you can check your local gym or a community center to see if there are any on offer. Alternatively, you can take classes online, either live through video calling software like Zoom, or by following along with videos posted on YouTube.

## Herbal Medicine

Like essential oils, herbal medicines are made from plant extracts and they have been used by different cultures for centuries. Lots of people take the view that herbal medicines don't really work, but around 40-70% of the mainstream medicines we use—like aspirin, morphine, and some cancer treatments—are derived from traditional herbal remedies (Chapman, 2023). Although you don't need a prescription for herbal remedies, it can be useful to talk to an herbalist who can help you choose the right medicine for you, taking into account any allergies or other medication that you're taking. A lot of herbal medicines react badly with common drugs like antidepressants or the contraceptive pill, so you should always do your research before picking something out.

Recommended herbal medicines to treat mental health issues include St. John's Wort (depression), passionflower (anxiety), and chamomile, but remember to check for interactions with any medication you're already taking if you decide to give them a try. You can get herbal medicines as capsules, liquid drops, teas, and creams. Many are available in health food stores, herbalists, or even some chain pharmacies and supermarkets.

**Meditation**

Meditation can help to empty your brain of unwanted and unhelpful thoughts. This is especially helpful if you find yourself often plagued with obsessive thoughts or if you struggle to wind down and get to sleep in the evening. You can get a number of different meditation apps for your mobile phone that will play relaxing music or prerecorded sessions to guide you through a calming meditation. You might also be able to find albums and tracks on music streaming services—really handy if you already have an account.

You can get different types of meditation, but most of them work by focusing your thoughts onto something—like your breathing or the sounds you can hear—which works to dispel any disruptive thoughts and stops them from taking over. Here are three simple meditation methods that you can used to relax:

- You can meditate by concentrating on your breathing. Count from one to five in your head while breathing in and then one to five again while breathing out. Another popular breathing exercise is called square breathing: breathe in, hold, breathe out, hold, doing each one for a count of four.

- Mindfulness meditation grounds you in the moment by getting you to meditate on your current surroundings and the sensations you are experiencing. Sit yourself somewhere comfortable and quiet and close your eyes. Try and focus in on different sounds you can hear and notice if they are close by or far away. Then focus on the different things you can feel: surfaces beneath your hands and feet, your clothing, the sun, or a breeze on your face.

- Find a track that plays the sounds of somewhere you can imagine, like waves on the beach. Close your eyes and imagine you are there. Try to fill in all the sensations: the feeling of the sand and the sun, the sight of the waves, palm trees, and an empty beach. Imagine yourself walking through your setting and relaxing. You can also do this with a river or forest scene, gentle jungle sounds, or even just the sound of rain.

**Light Therapy**

Some people suffer from a particular form of depression called Seasonal Affective Disorder (SAD), which is caused by the reduced hours of sunlight in the winter months. SAD can sometimes be treated by light therapy that involves spending an hour each day sitting in front of a special light called a light box. It is designed to replicate sunlight more closely than a normal light bulb and if you use it each morning it can help you to feel less depressed throughout the day.

SAD lamps and light boxes work by increasing the serotonin in your brain and reducing the levels of melatonin. This should make you feel happier and less sleepy. SAD can be treated with all the same medications and talk therapies as other forms of depression too, but lots of sufferers find that the light box significantly improves their mood.

You can buy light boxes online, but do make sure that they are medically approved and certified for the treatment of SAD, otherwise they won't be as effective. Some medications, like St. John's Wort and antipsychotics, don't react well to light treatment, so you should always speak to your doctor to make sure light therapy is safe and appropriate for you to try.

## Pet Therapy

Spending time with animals is known to make you feel happier. Stroking them is calming, exercising with them helps you to be more active, and some people find it easier to bond with animals than other people, especially if they've experienced a lot of trauma in their past. Lots of different animals are used as therapy companions, but dogs, cats, and horses are the most common. Some animals are trained to provide therapy and they visit hospitals, schools, prisons, and retirement homes to help comfort the people who are there.

Of course, having your own pet—if this is something that is appropriate and possible—can be hugely rewarding and beneficial. For people struggling with depression who find it difficult to spend energy on themselves, having to walk, feed, and interact with a dog can give them the motivation they need to get out of bed on difficult days. Unless you have a particularly vocal and sarcastic parrot, animals don't judge you or make you feel bad about yourself; they're happy to see you whether you've had a shower recently or not. Sometimes that can be just the help you need.

If you don't have a pet of your own, perhaps you could offer to walk a neighbor's dog, offer your services as a pet sitter, or volunteer at a local shelter.

## Art Therapies

Art therapies are different from talk therapies because they help you express your thoughts and emotions if you find it difficult to put things into words. You don't need to be particularly creative or good at art, music, or drama; you just need to be willing to have a go. You can have private sessions or work in a group. Art therapies are usually recommended for people who struggle with more serious mental health disorders like schizophrenia or psychosis, but they can also be effective for anyone dealing with trauma and severe anxiety.

The different types of art therapies currently available are:

- Art therapy: In these sessions, you'll use different creative media to express yourself, such as paints, chalk, photographs, and clay. You might do something different each session or take a few weeks to work on a larger project. Your therapist probably won't tell you what to draw, but they might suggest you depict things that make you feel a certain way. They'll also encourage you to talk about your work and explain why you chose the colors, media, and subjects that you did.

- Dance therapy: This means using movements to help you feel more at ease and comfortable in your body. If you feel anxious about the way that you look, are trying to reconcile your self-image after an eating disorder, or are struggling to come to terms with a life-changing injury, this therapy can help you address those feelings.

- Drama therapy: You can use different characters to act out situations that make you anxious, or explore your thoughts and feelings around past traumatic events in a way that depersonalizes the situation. Some drama therapists also use puppets or masks to further help you feel removed enough from events to be able to analyze and resolve them. If you find your imagination is always creating things for you to be anxious about, drama therapy can help refocus it and direct it into a more positive creative experience.

- Music therapy: This can involve listening to or creating music using simple instruments that you don't need to be skilled to play. These might be drums, cymbals, maracas, bells, or your own voice. Making different sounds can help to relieve tension and stress, and playing as part of a group will help you feel connected to others. If you find it difficult to make friends or feel like you fit in with other people, then joining a group music therapy session can help you learn how to work together with people and feel like you're part of a wider purpose.

## How to Help Yourself

It's all well and good showing you a dozen different ways to feel better, but one of the most debilitating symptoms of low mental health is a lack of energy. If you struggle to have enough energy to get up in the morning, how are you going to have the energy to go for a nature walk, write in your journal, do your homework from your CBT session, and meditate before bed?

The trick is to take it slow. Recognize that you can't change everything at once and give yourself permission to take baby steps. And if that's too much, snail steps will do.

## Taking a Mental Health Day

Sometimes we all need a vacation from our daily commitments and the problems that are plaguing us. Plan a day for yourself where you pause all your worries and stresses and focus on yourself. Explain to your caregivers that you need a day to decompress and tell them what they can do to help—keeping noisy siblings away and letting you off chores for the day would make a big difference.

Decide what you want to do, but try and stay away from social media and interactions with friends. Today is just about you. Some people like to catch up on things they don't usually have time for, like sorting out their room and decluttering. Others want to indulge, like taking a long bath and reading a book in peace. If all you have the energy for is staying in your pjs and watching reruns of reality television shows, that's fine too! The main aim of the day is to enjoy yourself and relax without worrying that you should be studying, helping friends, or spending all your energy on anyone other than yourself.

## Make Mental Health a Routine

The best way to look after your mental health is to add little bits to your daily routine, just like having breakfast or brushing your teeth. Choose a time of day when you know you can take five minutes to do something that centers on your mental health. Not only will this help to improve it, but you should keep it up even when you're feeling good—after all, you don't only brush your teeth when you have a cavity; you do it every day to prevent problems.

Here are some ideas for ways that you can slip mental health management into your everyday routine:

- Do five minutes of yoga when you get up.
- Massage an essential oil into your neck and shoulders before you get dressed.
- Have your breakfast outside or by the window so you can enjoy nature.
- Listen to a wellness podcast on the way to school.
- Choose a lunch with more leafy greens and less processed food.
- Walk home from school or get off the bus a couple of stops earlier.
- Dance to two upbeat songs.
- Write a plan for the week, adding all your homework and project deadlines, study time, and extracurricular activities.
- Cuddle or groom a pet.

# TEENS' GUIDE TO HEALTH AND MENTAL WELL...

- Write in your journal or complete an exercise in a DBT workbook.

- Read a chapter of a book.

- Meditate before bed.

Each of these activities only takes a few minutes. Pick one to start with and do it at the same time every day for two weeks, then add another. It's okay to swap one out if you've tried it and it doesn't sit right. I find it difficult to write my thoughts down in a journal, but I love meditating, so that's the activity I've chosen for my nightly routine. You're much more likely to stick with a new routine if you enjoy it and find it beneficial, so take the time to try different things.

# Chapter Eight

## The Importance of Hobbies

*We are not our trauma. We are not our brain chemistry. That's part of who we are, but we're so much more than that.*
–Sam J. Miller

So far we've spent a lot of time talking about what you can do to improve your mental health when it's failing, and looked at a lot of different mental health disorders that are common in teenagers. However, you shouldn't only give your mental health some attention when it's failing. You can't prevent every mental health slip, especially if you have an anxiety disorder or a major depressive episode, but there are a lot of things you can do to help yourself feel better on a day-to-day basis.

Having hobbies that you enjoy, socializing with people who make you feel good about yourself, and succeeding in completing tasks are all activities that give you boosts of serotonin and dopamine and keep your mood elevated. Having a positive mood, a good outlook, and a supportive friendship group all make it less likely that you will sink into a state of depression. However, I know that not everyone finds socializing easy, or has found groups local to them that they can join, so this chapter is designed to give you some ideas about ways to improve your mental health by having fun!

## How to Keep Your Mental Health in Good Shape

It's easier than you think to build a good habit. Look how many you already have: You (hopefully) schedule regular meal times, brush your teeth twice a day, shower regularly, and (again, hopefully) change your underwear on a daily basis. These are all habits that you do without really thinking about, and if you missed one of them, you'd probably feel weird and a little gross. Doing them regularly contributes to your good physical health.

I bet you probably have more bad mental health habits than good ones, like scrolling through social media for no reason, checking up on an ex's posts, eating the whole packet of cookies, staying up too late, and avoiding social situations. Doing these things on a daily basis can slowly erode your mental health and lead to you feeling depressed or anxious.

What's the solution? Do a little something each day that makes you feel happy. Having a hobby is a great way to do this. Hobbies are activities you do just because you enjoy them. Many of them have other benefits too, like helping you to meet new people or keep fit. Doing something you enjoy triggers the reward center of your brain, giving you a hit of dopamine. This feels good and makes you want to do that activity again, building a cycle of reward and repeat.

Having a regular hobby also reduces stress by keeping your cortisol levels down (Parkhurst, 2021). You don't even need to be good at it; you can be a master knitter or get all your yarn in a twist—it doesn't matter, as long as you have fun doing it.

## Let's Find You a Hobby!

One of the best ways to get into a hobby is to choose something linked to an interest you already have. For example, if you enjoy listening to music, maybe you could start learning an instrument, or if you already play, join a local band or orchestra. If that's not in your skill set, then why not support some local musicians and check out open mike nights or gigs. Not only will you have a great time and discover some new music, but you'll also meet some new, like-minded people.

## Solo hobbies

Hobbies don't have to be done in groups or be loud and active. Lots of people enjoy reading or listening to audiobooks and podcasts. You could also try your hand at writing short stories or poems—doing something creative is often especially rewarding.

Building a collection can also be really interesting and rewarding, and you can choose to collect anything that interests you. Popular collectibles include baseball cards, Pokémon cards, stamps, foreign coins, comic books, and Funko Pop figures.

If you like being outside, you could try your hand at gardening. You don't even need access to a huge open space. You can grow herbs, succulents, orchids, and other pot plants on a windowsill. Some fruits and vegetables that are easy for beginners to grow include chili peppers, strawberries, and tomatoes—all can be grown in the ground, in containers, or even in hanging baskets.

Cooking is another hobby that's easy to get started with and has lots of benefits. There are loads of YouTube and Instagram accounts that post recipes and meal ideas for you to cook along with at home. Now is a great time to start to learn to cook healthy meals for yourself and learn what makes up a balanced diet.

## Group Hobbies

Since the Netflix series *Stranger Things* became a big hit, Dungeons & Dragons has seen a resurgence in popularity. You can play in person or online and you can buy ready-planned adventure books with missions for your group, or you can plan your own. All you need is a couple of people, some dice, and a lot of imagination. It's a great way to socialize and meet new people; just look up your local gaming store to see if they have any groups looking for new members.

Board game nights are also good for trying new things and meeting new people. Modern board games have come a long way since Scrabble and Monopoly, and you can find everything from advanced strategy games to silly, party fun. Why not take it in turns with your friends to host a game night? You arrange the game and they all bring the snacks.

You can make the same arrangement with a movie night. Pick your favorite film to introduce your friends to. You might also find that your local movie theater will host cut-price teen screenings, or your religious community, school, or community center could have a monthly movie

## TEENS' GUIDE TO HEALTH AND MENTAL WELL...

showing. Go with a group or go on your own and meet other people with similar tastes to your own.

Of course, there are a whole host of community and school sports teams you could join. Some will be for serious competitors, whereas others will welcome people of all skills and abilities. This could be your chance to return to a sport you used to play or pick up something new.

Your local community center or gym will have a number of classes that would be appropriate for teens to join too. You could have a go at salsa dancing, kickboxing, or try a bit of tai chi. Some classes will just let you turn up when you can, but others will need you to book a course starting on a set date. You should be able to find information about these from the centers themselves, or on their web pages.

# Chapter Nine

# Recognizing Warning Signs

*Anything that's human is mentionable, and anything that is mentionable can be more manageable. When we can talk about our feelings, they become less overwhelming, less upsetting, and less scary.* –Fred Rogers

The more we talk about our mental health, the more it normalizes the conversation. A couple of generations ago, no one spoke about depression, stress, or anxiety; instead, people just carried on feeling low and not knowing why or what to do about it. There have been a few advertising campaigns over the last few years that have encouraged people to take a few minutes to check in with their friends and see if they're doing okay. Sometimes that's all it takes to make someone feel as if they matter.

## You're Not a Mind Reader

When a friend has a mental health episode, it's natural to wonder if you should have spotted the signs or worked out that they were struggling. The truth is, no matter how close you are, you can't always tell how they're feeling. Some people are really good at keeping secrets or hiding their true feelings, especially if it's something they've been doing for a long time. I speak from experience because it's something I did for most of my life. I was afraid and ashamed to let any of my friends or colleagues know that I wasn't coping—they all seemed to be doing fine, so why wasn't I? However, once I started talking about how I really felt, I was surprised how many other people opened up to me about the negative thoughts they were having. I thought I was the only person experiencing mental health problems; I didn't spot any signs that my friends were too.

You can't always tell from people's behavior or personality either. The really quiet kid might not be withdrawn; they might just be comfortable with their own company and not feel the need to seek attention. The popular kid might be really confident, or they might be overcompensating for feelings of anxiety about not being good enough.

What is often a good indicator that something isn't right, is when a friend's behavior changes. We can all have days where we don't feel like ourselves, but a shift in the way they act that lasts for a while probably means they have something on their mind. It could be that they're worried about things at home, they're considering quitting the team, or they've had a serious falling out with a friend, or it could mean that they have low mental health and it's beginning to affect how they feel.

The same is true for yourself. You should never feel upset or guilty that you didn't spot your mental health was declining. We all use our brains without really thinking about what's going on up there. Can you explain how your phone works? Probably not, but that doesn't stop you from being able to use it for loads of different things. Sometimes you might get an app that breaks, your phone battery might stop charging properly, or you could accidentally download a virus, and similar things can happen in your brain without you really understanding how it happened: A chemical imbalance, anxious thoughts, or a bout of depression can seem to come out of nowhere, and with no warning.

## Checking In Checklist

We're all much better at analyzing and diagnosing things our friends do than we are at looking at ourselves. Ever had to check your own essay at school and missed loads of typos and errors, but then had your friend find them the first time? It's the same with your mental health. If all teens were better educated on what a mental health crisis looked like, and how to check in with someone you think is struggling, you could all be such an amazing support network for each other. This is an age where you all put much more value on your peers' opinions than you do on adults', so how powerful would it be if you opened your DMs to find half a dozen messages from people saying "I've noticed your last couple of posts have been a bit sad. What can I do to help?"

With that in mind, here is a checklist of some of the most common signs of declining mental health. You can use it to keep an eye on your friends, or as a resource to help you spot when your own mental health is starting to fail. It's not always easy to know why you're feeling a certain way—after all, feeling tired could mean you stayed up too late on your Xbox, or it could be a symptom of depression—but if you spot that a couple of the following statements are true for you, it might be worth speaking to your family doctor.

Signs that someone has low mental health:

- They seem to be more sad than usual.
- They lack the energy to do normal activities and are always complaining of feeling tired or ex-

hausted.

- They space out, don't focus on conversations, and need you to repeat things.
- They lack enthusiasm for activities that they would have previously enjoyed.
- They cancel plans to meet up more often than normal or decline invitations to socialize.
- They suddenly ignore their friends and make new friends, with no triggering incident.
- They are sleeping more—maybe even napping at school or drifting off in class—or sleeping less.
- They lose interest in schoolwork, no longer seem motivated, and their grades start to slip.
- They have become more aggressive and are quick to anger.
- They suddenly have boundless energy and find it difficult to sit still or focus on a task.
- They are eating more or less than they did before, or eating in secret.
- They are suddenly more interested in sexual activities and may intensely pursue any opportunity.

- They show signs of self-harming—cuts, bruises, and burns—or suddenly refuse to bare their arms and legs or get undressed for games or lessons.

- They seem uninterested in planning for or talking about the future or make comments about there being no point in them doing so.

Conclusion

Remember, having mental health issues is not a sign of weakness, failure, or inadequacy. It is a sign of being human. We all have emotions and feelings, and we react to different situations in different ways. Some things are going to upset you; others will delight you. Some situations will make you worried where other people remain calm, and some will stress others out, but you will thrive.

I truly hope you have read through this book and found that nothing has sounded familiar, because that means you are probably doing a fantastic job of maintaining good mental health. However, I suspect that the majority of you are reading this because you already know that your mental health is suffering. In that case, I hope that you have found some understanding and come away with the knowledge that there is nothing wrong with you because you are finding life a little more difficult these days.

If you are ready to reach out for support, I hope you have found the confidence to do so, but if not, there is enough information in these pages that you can start to research ways to help yourself. Mental health is such a new area of wellness that new therapies and medications are hitting the market every year, so if you haven't found the right fit just yet, it might not be too long before it comes around.

The same is true for mental health disorders. It was not that long ago—the 1970s in fact—that depression was first recognized as a disorder, and now there are almost a dozen different variants and sub-types, each with their own distinct symptoms and treatments. The more research is done, the more categories of mental health issues are being developed, and the easier it is to diagnose when someone is suffering from something severe. The point is, if life seems unbearable right now, there is probably a diagnosable reason for it, and you should never give up hope that things will get better.

## Keeping Up Momentum

You wouldn't expect to be able to run a marathon without any training, and if you stopped playing football last year, you'd expect to be a little rusty if you suddenly picked it up again now. We all understand that you need to keep up a certain level of physical activity in order to maintain your fitness level, and it's exactly the same case

# TEENS' GUIDE TO HEALTH AND MENTAL WELL...

with your mental health. If you manage to recover from a crisis, the best way to make sure that you keep your mental health in good condition is to keep up the good practice. Don't ditch the journal if it helps you to reflect on your thoughts, keep up the bedtime yoga routine if it helps you fall asleep easier, and make that weekend morning run a permanent fixture in your mental fitness routine. It might seem like a lot of work now, but you'll thank yourself for it when you're older. Getting through your teenage years can feel like an uphill battle, but get it right, and you will emerge as the best, most resilient version of yourself, able to take on everything the adult world throws at you.

\*\*\*

*"Thank you for completing this book. If you've found it helpful, please consider leaving an honest review on your Amazon store, which will be appreciated by others.*
*Thank you,*
*Kev"*

**Teens' Guide to Health and Mental Wellness**

Click here

Thank you for your review

**Teens' Guide to Health and Mental Wellness**

Click here

Thank you for your review

# A Final Word

*A*FTER A WHILE, YOU *learn to ignore the names people call you and just trust who you are.* –Shrek

Your teenage years are like a storm. Everything you've ever known gets blown around and turned upside down. Some people find storms exciting—they chase lightning and set up equipment to record every moment—but for most of us, storms are scary and disorientating, leaving us hiding under the covers or even taking refuge in the cellar. Once it's over, you might not want to come out from your hiding place because you know the world will look different.

We all need a little help from time to time. Help realizing that a lot of the new feelings and emotions you're experiencing are due to puberty and are a perfectly normal, if unpleasant, stage of life. Help understanding how to make the most of your best qualities so that others see who you really are. Help learning how to cope when everything seems too much, so you have some useful tools to get you through stressful situations.

Until you try something, you won't know how well it works for you. You might think that some of the tips and messages in this book don't apply to you, while others will turn out to be just the help you needed. I know that breathing exercises and visualizing a conversation in your head might sound silly, but so do a lot of everyday activities if you had to explain them to someone who had never done them before. If you decide to try anything new, go into it with an open mind and the belief that it will work. You might just surprise yourself.

One of the reasons why grown ups have such a difficult time relating to teenagers is that they don't remember what it felt like to be one. You too will forget that sinking feeling of being picked last for a group project, the horror of realizing you need to read an essay out loud without a friendly face to focus on, and the way that your stomach flips when you're about to talk to someone for the first time. Teenagers feel every emotion with a fiery intensity, but this phase is short-lived, and so is the pain.

Perhaps the biggest takeaway from this book should be that adolescence is a phase that will pass. You might feel awkward, self-conscious, and anxious now, but that doesn't mean you will feel the same way for the rest of your life. Once your brain has finished rewiring itself, a lot of these issues will fade away, and if they don't, there are medical professionals you can talk to who will be able to offer you treatments for depression, anxiety, stress, and more.

But in the meantime, go out and find your people, the people who love you for who you are, who build you up and make you feel like you can achieve anything as long as you do it together. Because everyone deserves friends like that, including you.

## Free books you may find interesting...

**Teens' Guide to Overcoming Shyness**

Teens' Guide to
Overcoming Shyness

**Grown Up's Guide to Communicating With Teens**

Click

Grown Up's Guide to
Communicating With Teens

# About the Author

Having a stark choice of fighting teens on the city streets or helping them find their way in life, Kev Chilton knew which way he wanted to go!

For most of his working life, he was an inner-city cop and detective, concentrating on murder, gun crime, and other serious offences.

However, he joined the police as a 16-year-old cadet and early in his career, he was tasked with helping young offenders, which quickly became his speciality. He noticed that by simply listening to the problems young people were concerned with, the majority were prepared to listen to him back. He built trusting relationships with most, who were happy to listen to and act on his advice. Many responded positively, and they moved confidently into adulthood.

Throughout his police service, he arranged youth clubs, attended schools where he gave talks and maintained an open-door policy, encouraging any young person with a problem to approach him privately afterwards. He also set up and operated specialist juvenile squads geared towards helping those who had gone off the rails. The results were excellent, and he was never happier in his job than when he could redirect a young person's life onto the right path.

It was a fulfilling time in his life, and it helped him understand the constantly evolving challenges teenagers face as they transition to adulthood. More specifically, as times change, so do the needs and circumstances of young people. Choosing the path of mentorship over the chaos of city streets, he has dedicated his journey to helping teenagers, steering them away from conflict and towards a brighter future.

Through a series of empowering 'How-to' guidebooks for teens, Chilton has become a beacon of support for them.

Today, he is proud to utilise his extensive experience to make a positive impact. He is particularly attuned to the unique issues that young people are currently grappling with, and one of his goals is to bridge the gap between them and the adults in their lives.

He lives in a cold barn out in the country where he constantly fights the elements—a losing battle that keeps him off the streets!

# TEENS' GUIDE TO HEALTH AND MENTAL WELL...

### ***

**To learn more of the Teens' Guide Series, chat with the author and find more information about the amazing community he is building, visit his website at:**

**Teens' Guide Series Website**

Website
Click here

# **Dedication**

With special thanks to Beth, whose initial conversations guided my journey to create this five-book series.

Also, a special thanks to Grace for her meticulous research and invaluable advice, which played a pivotal role in creating the final product.

And to my good friend, Anna, who kept me sane throughout!

# TEENS' GUIDE TO HEALTH AND MENTAL WELL...

# Resources

If you want to find out more about what you have read in this book, you can find a wealth of information online, aimed at both UK and US audiences, as well as some that are accessible from anywhere in the world. I've tried to gather as many resources as I can that are aimed at teenagers, but there are some in here that are too good not to mention, even though they're aimed at a wider age range.

**Well-Being Directory**

**Behavioral**

**Therapies**

If you're looking for worksheets to help you manage your mental health, the website Therapist Aid is a great place

# TEENS' GUIDE TO HEALTH AND MENTAL WELL...

to find free downloads. You can filter the worksheets by age and by topic to help you find the best ones for your needs.

https://www.therapistaid.com/therapy-worksheets/

For CBT, you can find accredited CBT Therapists near you by visiting:

- (UK) https://babcp.com/CBTRegister
- (UK) https://www.bps.org.uk/find-psychologist
- (US) https://services.abct.org

If you are based in the UK, you can access different therapies through the NHS:

For general information on what support is out there and how to access support, visit .

## General Mental Health Support

For all things mental health-related in the UK, check out https://www.mind.org.uk.

Globally, offers DBT aimed at teens with courses running on a weekly basis and is available online from anywhere in the world.

Additionally, offers a range of information about mental health issues and eating disorders; to access the information, click on "For the public" and use the drop-down menu.

## Art Therapies

In the UK, visit .

In the USA, check out .

## Exercise and Mindfulness

Though not aimed at teens, is a great resource for all levels and can be accessed from anywhere in the world.

In the UK, the Couch to 5k program is extremely popular for getting people into running. There is a website——and an app available for iPhone and Android.

Did meditation and mindfulness sound like something you would like to try? The following site has lots of information for you, including some great beginner meditations that are recorded on audio files: .

For additional worksheets and resources on mindfulness, worry, and well-being, check out .

Additional information about exercising and its impact on stress and anxiety can be found here; .

For more information about exercise and depression, take a look at.

## Online Forums and Peer Support

For information, resources, and the opportunity to chat online with trained volunteers, visit https://www.themix.org.uk/.

If you're worried about asking for help, you can get information about what questions to ask, what your doctor will want to walk about, and what you can expect as a follow-up here: http://www.docready.org/#/home.

UK-based telephone, email, webchat, and text services for young people that will guide you to the right support can be found here: https://www.getconnected.org.uk/.

For online articles, forums, and peer-to-peer mental health support that you can access from a mobile, tablet, or desktop, visit: https://www.kooth.com/.

Here's a USA-based site with information about helplines and peer support groups, as well as positive social media accounts to follow and apps to download: https://onlineteenhelp.com/.

Finally, here are a couple of USA-based directories of support groups and therapists: https://support.therapytribe.com/teen-support-group/ and https://www.livewell-foundation.org/.

# References

Akers, A. (2022, March 25). *Why is Gen Z depressed?* Medical News Today. https://www.medicalnewstoday.com/articles/why-is-gen-z-depressed

Alban, D. (2018, June 27). *Serotonin vs Dopamine and Their Roles in Depression*. Be Brain Fit. https://bebrainfit.com/serotonin-dopamine/

American Psychological Association. (2018, November 1). *Stress Effects on the Body*. https://www.apa.org/topics/stress/body

Avendano, K. (2022, April 29). *40 Inspirational Mental Health Quotes*. Good Housekeeping. https://www.goodhousekeeping.com/life/a39739060/mental-health-quotes/

BBFC. (2021, September 20). *Teens' three biggest mental health concerns revealed by new BBFC research*. BBFC. https://www.bbfc.co.uk/about-us/news/teens-three-big

gest-mental-health-concerns-revealed-by-new-bbfc-research

Bennington-Castro, J. (2018, February 1). *Which Medication Is Best for Treatment of Depression? | Everyday Health*. EverydayHealth.com. https://www.everydayhealth.com/depression/guide/medications

Canadian Mental Health Association. (2013). *Depression*. https://www.heretohelp.bc.ca/infosheet/depression

Canadian Mental Health Association. (2015). *What's the difference between sadness and depression?* https://www.heretohelp.bc.ca/q-and-a/whats-the-difference-between-sadness-and-depression

Centers for Disease Control and Prevention. (2019). *Adolescent Health*. https://www.cdc.gov/nchs/fastats/adolescent-health.htm

Chapman, K. (2023, May 15). *Education in chemistry*. Royal Society of Chemistry. https://edu.rsc.org/feature/from-traditional-remedies-to-modern-medicines/4017426.article

Chung, R. (2019, November 9). *Mental Health and Teens: Watch for Danger Signs*. HealthyChildren.org. https://www.healthychildren.org/English/ages-stages/teen/Pages/Mental-Health-and-Teens-Watch-for-Danger-Signs.aspx

Cleveland Clinic. (2021, December 10). *Cortisol*. https://my.clevelandclinic.org/health/articles/22187-cortisol

DeWitt, H. (2022, December 5). *What Are Unhealthy Coping Mechanisms?* Thriveworks. https://thriveworks.com/help-with/coping-skills/unhealthy-coping-mechanisms/

Drinkaware. (2021). *Alcohol and Depression.* https://www.drinkaware.co.uk/facts/health-effects-of-alcohol/mental-health/alcohol-and-depression

Dziurkowska, E., & Wesolowski, M. (2021). Cortisol as a Biomarker of Mental Disorder Severity. *Journal of Clinical Medicine, 10*(21), 5204. https://doi.org/10.3390/jcm10215204

Faculty of Public Health. (n.d.). *Concepts of Mental and Social Wellbeing.* https://www.fph.org.uk/policy-advocacy/special-interest-groups/special-interest-groups-list/public-mental-health-special-interest-group/better-mental-health-for-all/concepts-of-mental-and-social-wellbeing/

familydoctor.org. (1996, June). *Types of Antidepressants.* https://familydoctor.org/types-of-antidepressants/

Fasihi Harandi, T., Mohammad Taghinasab, M., & Dehghan Nayeri, T. (2017). The correlation of social support with mental health: A meta-analysis. *Electronic Physician, 9*(9), 5212–5222. https://doi.org/10.19082/5212

Hirschlag, A. (2020, December 19). Do You Live with Anxiety? Here Are 11 Ways to Cope. Healthline. https://www.healthline.com/health/mental-health/how-to-cope-with-anxiety

Kaiser, E. (2021, May 1). *11 Mental Health Quotes For Kids - Mental Health Awareness Month*. Better Kids. https://betterkids.education/blog/11-mental-health-quotes-for-kids-mental-health-awareness-month

Kapil, R. (2019, July 11). *Four Ways Culture Impacts Mental Health*. Mental Health First Aid. https://www.mentalhealthfirstaid.org/2019/07/four-ways-culture-impacts-mental-health/

Kids Health. (2002, June). Helping Teens Who Cut (for Parents). https://kidshealth.org/en/parents/help-cutting.html

Leamey, T. (2023, March 20). *These 8 Hobbies Will Help Your Mental Health Spring Forward*. CNET. https://www.cnet.com/health/mental/these-8-hobbies-will-help-your-mental-health-spring-forward/

London, C. (2023). *Understanding genetic contributions to mental health*. Maudsley Biomedical Research Center. https://www.maudsleybrc.nihr.ac.uk/stories-of-research/understanding-genetic-contributions-to-mental-health/

Lyness, D. (2019). 10 *Ways to Manage Everyday Stress*. Teens Health. https://kidshealth.org/en/teens/stress-tips.html

McCabe, C. (2021, February 11). *The Science Behind Why Hobbies Can Improve Our Mental Health*. The Conversation. https://theconversation.com/the-science-behind-why-hobbies-can-improve-our-mental-health-153828

McCarthy, C. (2019, November 20). *Anxiety in Teens is Rising: What's Going On?* HealthyChildren.org. https://www.healthychildren.org/English/health-issues/conditions/emotional-problems/Pages/Anxiety-Disorders.aspx

McCarthy, C. (2022, April 21). *Eating disorders spike among children and teens: What parents should know*. Harvard Health. https://www.health.harvard.edu/blog/eating-disorders-spike-among-children-and-teens-what-parents-should-know-202204212731

Mental Health First Aid. (2020, August 6). *The Importance of Having a Support System*. https://www.mentalhealthfirstaid.org/2020/08/the-importance-of-having-a-support-system/

Mental Health Foundation. (2021, September 17). *Stress*. https://www.mentalhealth.org.uk/explore-mental-health/a-z-topics/stress

Mental Health Foundation. (2022). *About Mental Health*. https://www.mentalhealth.org.uk/explore-mental-health/about-mental-health

MHA. (2021, June 7). *The Benefits of Aromatherapy*. Mental Health Association in Delaware. https://www.mhainde.org/the-benefits-of-aromatherapy/

Mind. (2019, March). *Physical Activity and Your Mental Health*. Www.mind.org.uk. https://www.mind.org.uk/information-support/tips-for-everyday-living/physical-activity-and-your-mental-health/about-physical-activity/

Mind. (2021a, February). *About anxiety*. https://www.mind.org.uk/information-support/types-of-mental-health-problems/anxiety-and-panic-attacks/about-anxiety/

Mind. (2021b, October). *What Are Arts and Creative Therapies?* https://www.mind.org.uk/information-support/drugs-and-treatments/talking-therapy-and-counselling/arts-and-creative-therapies/

Mind. (2023). *Facts and figures about young people and mental health*. https://www.mind.org.uk/about-us/our-strategy/doing-more-for-young-people/facts-and-figures-about-young-people-and-mental-health/

Mindful. (2019, April 13). *How to meditate*. https://www.mindful.org/how-to-meditate/

Moore, M. (2016, May 17). *What's the Difference Between CBT & DBT?* Psych Central. https://psychcentral.com/lib/whats-the-difference-between-cbt-and-dbt

Morin, A. (2019). *Simple Ways to Improve Your Psychological Well-Being*. Verywell Mind. https://www.verywellmind.com/improve-psychological-well-being-4177330

Murdoch Children's Media. (2021, October 29). *Children with mental health problems at increased risk of mental disorders as adults.* Murdoch Children's Research Institute.
https://www.mcri.edu.au/news-stories/children-mental-health-problems-increased-risk-mental-disorders-adults

National Alliance on Mental Illness. (2023, April). *Mental health by the numbers*. https://www.nami.org/mhstats

Nemours Teens Health. (2018). *Compulsive Exercise (for Teens)*. https://kidshealth.org/en/teens/compulsive-exercise.html

Neurosurgery. (2016, September 4). *How Brain Chemicals Influence Mood and Health*. UPMC HealthBeat. https://share.upmc.com/2016/09/about-brain-chemicals/

New World Encyclopedia. (n.d.). *Norepinephrine*. https://www.newworldencyclopedia.org/entry/Norepinephrine

NHS. (2021, February 12). *Treatment - Seasonal Affective Disorder (SAD)*. https://www.nhs.uk/mental-health/conditions/seasonal-affective-disorder-sad/treatment/

Parkhurst, E. (2021, October 25). *How hobbies improve mental health*. Utah State University. https://extension.usu.edu/mentalhealth/articles/how-hobbies-improve-mental-health

Peytrignet, S., Marszalek, K., Grimm, F., Thorlby, R., & Wagstaff, T. (2022, February 8). *Children and Young People's Mental Health*. The Health Foundation. https://www.health.org.uk/news-and-comment/charts-and-infographics/children-and-young-people-s-mental-health

Premier Health. (2017, September 28). *Anxiety, Depression, Stress: Why the Differences Matter*. https://www.premierhealth.com/your-health/articles/women-wisdom-wellness-/anxiety-depression-stress-why-the-differences-matter

Raising Children Network. (2022, October 19). *Stress and stress management: pre-teens and teenagers*. https://raisingchildren.net.au/pre-teens/mental-health-physical-health/stress-anxiety-depression/stress-in-tee ns#stress-management-for-pre-teens-and-teenagers-nav-title

ReachOut. (2015). *Stress and teenagers*. https://parents.au.reachout.com/common-concerns/everyday-issues/stress-and-teenagers

Rethink Mental illness. (2022). Complementary and Alternative Treatments for Mental Health. https://www.rethink.org/advice-and-information/living-with-mental-illness/treatment-and-support/complementary-and-alternative-treatments-for-mental-health/

Ritchie, D. (2021, June 17). *Sedentary Lifestyle: 10 Signs You Aren't Active Enough*. Calendar. https://www.calendar.com/blog/sedentary-lifestyle-10-signs-you-arent-active-enough/

Robinson, L., Smith, M., & Segal, J. (2023, August 14). *Depression Types, Causes, and Risk Factors.* Help Guide. https://www.helpguide.org/depression-types-causes-and-risk-factors.htm

Romeo, R. D. (2013). The Teenage Brain: The Stress Response and the Adolescent Brain. *Current Directions in Psychological Science, 22*(2), 140–145. https://doi.org/10.1177/0963721413475445

Rose Hill Center. (2019, December 9). Understanding the Stigma Around Antidepressants. https://www.rosehillcenter.org/mental-health-blog/understanding-the-stigma-around-antidepressants/

Sam, K. S. (2020, March 18). *Importance of Emotional Wellbeing for Overall Health*. Assurance. https://www.nhassurance.com/blog/importance-of-emotional-wellbeing-for-overall-health

Sawchuk, C. (2022, October 14). *Depression (major depressive disorder)*. Mayo Clinic. https://www.mayoclinic.org/diseases-conditions/depression/symptoms-causes/syc-20356007

Schlinger, A. (2023, July 21). *10 Signs You're Out of Shape*. The Healthy. https://www.thehealthy.com/exercise/how-to-tell-if-you-are-out-of-shape/

Shah, D. R. (2014, September 23). *10 Benefits Of Yoga For Teenagers And 13 Simple Poses*. Mom Junction. https://www.momjunction.com/articles/benefits-of-yoga-for-your-teenager_0094957/

Sharma, A., Madaan, V., & Petty, F. D. (2006). Exercise for mental health. *Primary Care Companion to the Journal of Clinical Psychiatry*, *8*(2), 106. https://www.ncbi.nlm.nih.gov/pmc/articles/PMC1470658/

Sinclair, J. (2021, February 15). *What is social well-being? Definition, types, and how to achieve it*. Better

Up. https://www.betterup.com/blog/what-is-social-well-being-definition-types-and-how-to-achieve-it

Smith, M., Robinson, L., & Segal, J. (2019, March 20). *Teenager's Guide to Depression*. HelpGuide.org. https://www.helpguide.org/articles/depression/teenagers-guide-to-depression.htm

Southside Medical Center. (2019, January 14). *How Brain Chemistry Affects Mental Health*. https://southsidemedical.net/how-brain-chemistry-affects-mental-health/

St John Ambulance. (n.d.). *Signs that someone may be experiencing poor mental health*. https://www.sja.org.uk/course-information/guidance-and-help/mental-health-resources/signs-that-someone-may-be-experiencing-poor-mental-health/

Therapist Aid. (n.d.-a). *Cognitive Restructuring: Decatastrophizing (Worksheet)*. https://www.therapistaid.com/therapy-worksheet/decatastrophizing/cbt/none

Therapist Aid. (n.d.-b). *Urge Surfing: Distress Tolerance Skill (Worksheet)*. https://www.therapistaid.com/therapy-worksheet/urge-surfing-handout

Vandenabeele, P. (2021, March 31). *What's the difference between anxiety and depression?* Bupa. https://www.bupa.co.uk/newsroom/ourviews/anxiety-depression

World Health Organization. (2021, November 17). *Mental health of adolescents*. https://www.who.int/news-room/fact-sheets/detail/adolescent-mental-health

Yassin, F. (2021, October 12). *5 Reasons Why Teenagers are Suffering from Anxiety Disorder More than Ever Before*. The Wave Clinic. https://thewaveclinic.com/blog/5-reasons-why-teenagers-are-suffering-from-anxiety-disorder-more-than-ever-before/

Young Minds. (2021). *Mental Health Statistics UK*. https://www.youngminds.org.uk/about-us/media-centre/mental-health-statistics/

www.ingramcontent.com/pod-product-compliance
Lightning Source LLC
Chambersburg PA
CBHW052140070526
44585CB00017B/1914